STEELHEAD & SALMON
Drift-Fishing Secrets

Timothy Kusherets

Dedication

I would like to dedicate this book to all fishermen that have the love and passion for the sport of drift fishing. The many driving questions and the insatiable need for the answers to those questions have greatly aided in the birth of this book.

To all the first-timer fishermen that allowed me to take them out into the field and show them what I know, I say thank you. In particular, I want to thank Mike Lajoy. Every teacher longs for a great student and, by far, you do me honor with your extensive knowledge in the sport of drift fishing by showing others what you have learned. Most importantly, it is my honor and privilege of both meeting and working with a man who has had the foresight to look into the future of the sport of drift fishing. Frank Amato is both a fine fisherman and a a gentleman, and I am better for having met him. Thank you for believing in me too.

Frank Amato Publications, Inc.

P.O. Box 82112, Portland, Oregon 97282

503.653.8108 • www.amatobooks.com

All photographs by the author unless otherwise noted.

Book & Cover Design: Kathy Johnson

Printed in Singapore

Softbound ISBN 13: 978-1-57188-300-1 • Softbound ISBN 10: 1-57188-300-2

UPC: 0-81127-00134-7

3 5 7 9 10 8 6 4 2

STEELHEAD & SALMON
Drift-Fishing Secrets

Timothy Kusherets

Frank Amato

PORTLAND

Contents

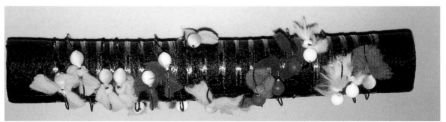

Preface

This book is the culmination of over 36,000 hours of research. The areas of research span marine biology, ichthyology, meteorology and physics as they apply to lunar cycles; water currents and sediment accumulation, topography, nautical charting, state and local government and that laws that govern fishing rights of the recreational and commercial fishermen; and environmental impact studies covering both salmon and steelhead that are hatchery-reared as the they apply to gill netting. I have also worked with the state hatcheries harvesting and tagging salmon.

The main premise for this book is anyone should be able to go out and enjoy the sport of drift fishing. I wrote this book for both the consummate professional and the novice. It is user-friendly and informative. If the reader just wants to know how put a fish on the hook immediately he or she can reference the first portion of the book. If the reader wants to know the reasons for the new-found abilities he or she can reference the extensive glossary at the back of the book, which will then go into very brief detail with each item.

One of the many things that motivated me to write this book were the incessant questions people had. They wanted to know why I was catching so many fish. There were some that were disgruntled, that I would be able to go down to the water that that they had been fishing since dawn and catch fish, within one or two casts, when they had caught none. I was always happy to answer any questions, but I knew I would never have enough time to tell everyone everything that they needed to know. Many of the questions were redundant and easily explained, but it was the tight-mouthed professionals who made it difficult for the laymen to get the information they needed. I wanted to know how to drift fish, but even the expert guides would not tell me all of the essential things I needed to know. I was told that it would take me a few years before I would understand enough of the associated nuances to be able to catch my first steelhead. The other "how to" books gave just enough information to motivate people to go out and fish, but didn't give enough detail that would allow people to understand what it was they had to do to catch fish and understand why they were catching fish if they did.

I had already been studying the habits of fish for many years and my determination to understand freshwater and marine life would not let me accept that only the good ole boys were privy to exchanging data and current information that would give them the edge on how to catch fish by drift fishing. The only thing left for me to do was to depend on my ability to research the recreational fishing industry and cross-reference what it knew with scientific applications. The end result of my research was the mystique and dogma clouded the industry, and that anything within it could be explained in easily understood terms.

The answers to some of the questions describe: what the "hit feels like; how to identify species of fish; essential gear; how to read water; the process of preparing to fish; when the fish will bite your hook; how to find the fish; when and where to go fishing; and how to predict weather and wind".

This book is also founded on the belief that the recreational fisherman will catch so many fish that it behooves us all to practice "catch and release."

How to use this book

The key to using this book is based on a simple premise. The information that all drift fishermen must have can be found in the body of the book with full explanations behind each subtitle. It can be broken down into two sections: fishermen that want to breeze through the book and locate specific items can reference the glossary towards the back of the book; it is there that brief explanations and definitions are found. It is the most extensive glossary of its kind; fishermen that want a thorough understanding can read the body of the book in its entirety. Each subtitle is covered as a vital component of the whole and should be read for the best edification. As the reader finds his or her way from the front to the back of the book they will find all the tools needed to compete with professionals, though rote practice is something highly recommended to successfully assimilate all the concepts.

As you read the book and find something in quotations you may not be familiar with you can turn to the back of the book for brief explanations in the alphabetized glossary. If you don't want to go to the back of the book you will be satisfied to know that all of the quoted remarks are explained in detail as you read on.

I will restate what has already been said. The best way to learn the many concepts is by repetitive study. Reading water and locating fish is something you will need to practice, that being the case, I have illustrated what to look for when you are looking at water with many photographs so you will be well armed when you go to the river to fish. With practice you will become adept at reading and decoding water in a very short period of time with the subsequent lessons to follow, which involve setting the hook, fighting fish, and landing them. There are other items in the book that should be considered when studying these concepts but do not let the material intimidate you. Drift fishing is remarkably easy and the most productive way to fish for steelhead and salmon.

Introduction

It was not an easy decision for me to become a drift fisherman. I had been fishing for salmon for a few years when a friend of mine told me about it. Ron Sullivan, my best friend, has long since gone to join the Coast Guard. He told me that he wanted a hitch with them so that when his tour of duty was over he could permanently move to Alaska to catch some of the legendary fish that he would never be able to catch down here in Washington.

Ron told me he was tired of catching chinook and cohos the same old way in the same old places. He wanted to go to the Puyallup River and try his hand at drift fishing. At his insistence, I went along. I wasn't sure as to how to take him, he spoke of drift fishing with a passion that I hadn't seen in him since he and I first met. I did go with him, but I brought my usual spinner baits hoping to catch the fish he was sure to miss with all this drift nonsense.

I was amazed at the water when we got there. It was high, muddy and fast. I had never fished in water like that. The surface of the water was a circus of movement that boggled my mind. I could see the backs of pinks, silvers, and kings all over the length and breadth of the river. All I could think about was getting my stuff into the water and catching some fish. I was set up in no time and cast out with a rooster-tail spinner and caught a pink on the first cast. Ron was fumbling around with his stuff and disgusted at my lack of enthusiasm to drift. I didn't care, I had gotten one on the first cast and that

put me ahead. Ron and I were constantly competing to see who could catch the most fish in the shortest amount of time. So there it was, I was ahead and he was angry. It was standard procedure for the both of us, one of us was always going to be disgruntled.

It wasn't long before he was about to put his line into the water. I wanted to see what he had done, and he was proud to show me his rig setup. Though he had professed to know what he was doing, and depending on my ignorance, which at the time was a good bet, he glowed as he pointed out the details of his mainline which consisted of twenty-pound test. His weight system was some sliding lead that amounted to about two ounces. His leader had a seventeen-pound test and was three feet long; he was using two size-eight corkies and a 3/0 treble hook. I didn't know then why, but I thought the whole thing was laughable. I was sure that the only thing that rig was capable of doing was snagging. He waded out into the muddy river until he was about thigh high, and fished current that had a back-eddy on the other side of the river. It looked as though it was a good place for fish to hold. Having no previous experience with that type of fishing, I stood there and watched as he cast out. The cast was straight out in front of him and it fell promptly to the bottom. He waited for something to happen. That section of river was moving moderately fast but his line defied the water, as it didn't move one inch. It had all of the trappings of plunking rather than drift fishing. A couple of minutes went by when I turned to him.

"Ron, what in the hell do you think you're doing? This isn't fishing. You're trying to snag fish. How stupid do you think the other fishermen around here are? Once they see your setup, they're going to call the game warden and we're going to go to jail."

"Do I tell you how to fish? No I don't. If you want to watch and learn something I don't mind, but if you're going to just complain, why don't you go down-river to fish?"

I moved down river approximately fifty yards. Catch and release was a great way to spend a Saturday. I had landed seven or eight fish when I heard him yell, "Fish On!" I couldn't believe it, he had gotten one. I ran upstream to see Ron holding onto his rod as though his life depended on it as a fish on the end of his line proceeded to haul ass up the river and not down, as most fish did. I had never seen anything like it. What in the river could pull on his line as though he had four-pound test and not the twenty that I knew that he had? Ron didn't say anything after his initial exaltation, but the look on his face said it all. The fish never came towards the surface to indicate that it might jump. The fight went on like that for about ten minutes until it started to minimize its pull, which allowed Ron to yard it back until he was finally able to tail a 23-pound king salmon. I thought the fight was spectacular and the means by which he caught the fish made me want to drift fish, but I couldn't help pointing out something that was weird.

"Hey, look at where the hook is."

The hook was in the crotch of the jaw, just like you would expect a good hookset to be, but the hook was on the "outside" of it as opposed to being on the inside.

"So what? The regulation handbook says that a snagged fish has to be put back, and as you can see the hook is in the mouth."

"Hey, I don't know who you think you're trying to kid, but I have a very good idea about what just happened. Ron, think about it for a moment. When this big bad boy came into the river his esophagus was completely closed, that meant that he was never going to eat again, right?"

"Yeah. What of it?"

"Well, then the only reason he would have for moving his mouth open and closed would be to wash water over his gills to get oxygen, and he probably did it more and more as his body matured as it began to necrotize. It just makes sense to me, anyway, that you snagged it on the outside of the mouth. Either way, you caught the fish fair and square and you snagged it all at the same time. I guess the only question is, what are you going to do with the fish?"

"Quit your griping, you're just jealous."

He strung up the fish and tied it to a root of a tree that was sticking out of the water near the bank. I liked Ron. He was my best friend, but I knew that the fish was snagged and he should've let it go. It was his moral dilemma and I couldn't interfere. I sat down on the bank and watched him go back to fishing. He had been at it for a short time when he hooked another one. He had cast out in the same spot, and the second fish that he hooked into did the exact same thing as the first one. I watched him for some time before he asked me to go up river and net the fish.

"Well, was the fish snagged this time?"

Ron seemed sure that he was right about this one, but he wasn't. It was snagged in the exact same way. I told him that if he kept this one I was going to leave, he did and I left. The trail that we had to go along to get to the river was about a mile long and our cars waited at the top of a very steep hill. I waited for him, but he never came. I was there for an hour before I left.

Ron and I didn't fish together many more times after that. He was a good man, and I miss him. But I was sure that he had figured out how to snag those fish. I couldn't prove it, but I remain stoic about that issue. Still, that day had its good points. I had never seen drift fishing before and I was intrigued.

I didn't believe that Ron had gone about it the right way and I needed to find out if I was right. I went to the nearest bookstore and began my investigation. The first few books I read were confusing, and contradicted each other as to how to drift fish. I knew a lot of people that fished for salmon and sought out those whom I perceived to be the best. I was told by each and every one of them that it would take a lot of time and effort to catch my first steelhead, which I thought was funny, because I would always start out by asking them about drift fishing and not steelhead. Very quickly I came to know that here in the Northwest that steelhead and drift fishing were synonymous. The more I investigated, the more my focus was directed at drift fishing for steelhead.

I recall that the only thing that made sense to me was to approach the issue scientifically. I could not accept the fact that it was going to take me years to catch my first steelhead. I knew intrinsically that all the supposed hardships that most fishermen go through could be reasoned out and overcome. I had to get to know the many problems first before I could defeat them.

One of the first things I had to embrace was that everyone I spoke with agreed that the typical strike of a steelhead was imperceptible. Most agreed that

the only way to overcome the lack of understanding was to watch your line and pull back each and every time that your line hesitated as it went through the drift. They believed that it was the only way to identify with certainty that a fish had tampered with the line. They also believed that the "mainline" and "leader" should be as invisible as possible. That meant both mainline and leader were going to be very hard to see for both the fish and the fisherman. The invisible line makes sense for the fish, but bothered me, because the fisherman needs to "see" the mainline. Something was not adding up, and the answer was not yet obvious.

One-third of a steelhead's brain is dedicated to it's olfactory sense. It's sense of smell is 5,000 times that of a human's. I imagine that it must be just about intense enough for it to "see" scents, as well as smell them. It stood to reason that a steelhead needed such a powerful ability because its instinct for survival demanded it. I believed that what I read was true, but I saw something else in the facts. One-third of that tiny brain was a very large percentage of any brain. I reasoned that a fish would have to be of very low intelligence if that were the case. I also believed that if the fish couldn't see the line that led to the offering, then it probably wouldn't care what color the mainline was or how visible it might be. Its main concern should be the offering and nothing else. All things being equal, the fish should bite at the "invisible" line and the fisherman should be able to see a "highly visible" line at the same time. It was that kind of reasoning and investigation that led me down a path of many discoveries about drift fishing which bear disclosing to all those who brave the woods, rivers, and weather to catch one of these elusive creatures.

At right is a photo of a man standing on the opposite shore of where Ron and I

had been fishing the morning I discovered drift fishing. Though the water is much higher than it had been when he and I had the fishing episode that I described to you, the water clarity is the very same that it was on that day.

When you go fishing, you sometimes meet the most interesting people. This man had a lot to say on how to catch coho salmon, which were running at the time that I took this photo. He told me something that made sense, though I have yet to try it myself. He had lived along the Puyallup River all of his life and the fishing was nothing like it used to be. He said that the river used to be the center of the universe when it came time to catch steelhead. In his youth he would go down to the river and put his arm in the water up to his elbow and wait until his limb became so cold that he could barely move. He would then go to a honey hole, not far from where he was, and reach down into the water and move his hand around very slowly until he could feel the tail wrist of a fish and slowly guide his palm over it. He was able to do it because his hand had become as cold as the water around it and the fish would disregard him, probably thinking he was a branch or something. He'd slowly make his hand tighter and tighter until he knew that he had to make a quick grab or the fish would violently swim away. Wrestling the fish, he would fling it up on the bank and go home, "and that is how you fish without a fishing rod." He said that he was too old to do it anymore, but he sure had a lot of fun doing it. I told him the story about my friend. Judd, the man in the picture, told me that it was the same kind of thinking that led to the downfall of so many species that used to prevail in that system. Judd said the river would never recover.

One of the things that I enjoy about fishing is meeting a man like this one. He had a wealth of experience that he wanted to share and I listened eagerly. Sadly though there are only so many hours in a day and we had to say goodbye.

Going out on the trips that I do, the fortune of meeting men who are willing to share their knowledge is a perk of the great adventure that is drift fishing.

11

Most Popular River Drift-Fishing Species

Chum have green and purple barbs the length of their bodies.

Coho have a hooked snout, most pronounced in the males.

Chinook Salmon

Chinook are the largest of the salmon family. Their spawning colors range from golden brown to pine green. All salmon have a forked tail.

Black mouth and gumline.

Spots on the entire tail.

Steelhead

Steelhead have a red stripe that begins at the gill plate and runs the length of the body along the lateral line. The stripe becomes darker as the fish get closer to the predetermined spawning cycle.

Anatomy

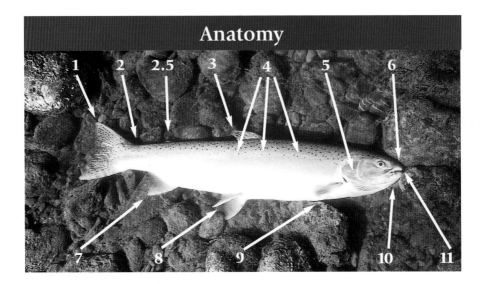

1. **Caudal fin,** or tail, is the primary source of forward propulsion. The spots, or lack of them, help to identify various species of salmon and steelhead.

2. **Peduncle,** or tail wrist. The area of the body a fisherman grabs when attempting to land a fish without a net. Under most conditions, grabbing a fish by the peduncle immobilizes it while you retrieve your hook.

2.5. **Adipose fin** is used as a means of identifying a native from a hatchery reared fish. A clipped fin (missing) indicates a hatchery fish, unclipped (present) identifies a native (for most areas).

3. **Dorsal fin** is the only fin that sits on the back of an anadramous fish. The dorsal-fin height is sometimes used to distinguish hatchery steelhead and natives when physical marking is not done.

4. **Lateral line** is a series of sensory pores along the head and sides of the fish by which water currents, vibrations, and pressure changes are perceived.

5. **Gill plate** protects the sensitive gills underneath.

6. **Nostrils** help locatie potential food, and are also used for migratory purposes. The olfactory capabilities of a salmon are 5000 times that of a human's.

7. **Anal-fin rays** identify anadromous species. Thirteen or more rays and the fish is a salmon, if there are twelve or less it's a trout.

8. **Ventral fins** are stabilizers and are also used in some areas for tracking purposes. Much like clipping the adipose fin, occasionally one of the ventral fins may be removed by state hatchery rearing ponds.

14

Female Gender Identification

The female upper jaw does not go past the eye

Male Gender Identification

The male upper jaw goes past the eye

9. Pectoral fins are the forefront fins. Fish can manipulate these fins for directional navigation. Though it's difficult, a fish can move backwards using them.

10. Mandible and kype (lower jaw) is distended and exaggerated during the spawning stages. It is the protrusion of the lower jaw that indicates that a male salmon has approached its final stages of maturation.

11. Maxillary, or upper jaw. The length of the maxillary helps to identify gender. If it goes past the orbits of the eyes it is a male, if it does not it is female.

15

Gear

Spinning Reel

One of the most important qualities a reel must have is a smooth drag. Infinite anti-reverse is a must for any reel. It stops the spool from back-lashing when it is time to set the hook and allows your drag to start working immediately. Reels that have infinite anti-reverse have a very smooth drag system, which, if set properly, will ensure that you will not lose the fish on the end of your line. The "spin ratio" from the spool to the handle should not be less than five to one. That is to say, the carriage around your spool should rotate five times for each single turn of your handle. The packages that house the reels will show the ratio to look like this, 5.0:1 ratio. The higher the ratio, the faster you will be able to reel in your line. This is extremely important when it comes time to fight the fish. On occasion after the fish has hit your line, it will run straight towards you or perhaps even up stream. If the fish is able to create enough

slack in your line it may be sufficient for it to throw your hook or snap your line. Understanding the gear ratio will help you in your need to better fight the fish. Okuma reels are the best value for your dollar.

Rod

Your fishing rod should have a length of no less than 8 1/2 feet up to 10 1/2 feet. For the purposes of this book we will concentrate on spin-casting rods. The eyes

guide the line influencing how much pressure will be placed on the line and reel, consequently, the more eyes the better. The more guides that you have, the less direct pressure is placed on the line, thus improving the chances that your line, reel, and rod will not be damaged. A good rule of thumb is one eye for every foot of the rod.

Rods come in different weight capability classes; there is ultra-light, medium, medium to heavy, and heavy actions, that translate into weight classes for the fish and line capacity. When fishing for steelhead you will need a medium to heavy action rod, less if you really want to fight for sport. The line test should be between ten and fourteen pounds. The lure casting weight should be from a minimum eighth of an ounce to half an ounce maximum.

Flexibility in a rod is an important factor. It is up to the angler to decide the desired rod flexibility and sensitivity. The more "sensitive" a rod is, the more flexible they tend to be. People who want a stiffer rod are looking for hook-setting power. There is a trade-off between the two that you will have to determine for yourself. There is nothing wrong with either stiff or flexible rods, but for the stiffer rods you sacrifice sensitivity for the hook- setting power that they offer, and

the flexible ones offer great sensitivity while at the same time sacrificing hook-setting power.

They can be found in two classifications, the first is a Fast-action tip. The tip is where you will find most of the flexibility but the rest of the rod will be stiff. Second is the Noodle Rod, that can be bent almost into an entire circle. Both are very capable of hooking and landing fish well over fifty pounds if you play the fish with patience.

The rod will also tell you what classification of line to use. The one that you see me using in the photo on the left states on the "blank" of the rod near the butt, that it is capable of using lines that range from eight-pound to twelve-pound test. If I were to go under the recommended test by using six pound or go over by using fourteen-pound test, the possibility of the line breaking, or the rod itself, becomes very real. Think about the species of fish you want to fish and how you will fight them, the difference between the two will help you in determining the kind of rod to get. I like to play the fish, but at the same time I want some strength in the rod, so I decided on the range that I talked about earlier which lies somewhere in the medium-action range. In the above photo you see me fighting a large chinook salmon; it didn't take as long as you might think with only ten-pound test.

Hooks

For each species of fish you encounter, you will have to adjust the kind of hook you use. Though the species does play a part in your choice, so does the fishing area. You will need to have your regulation handbook with you at all times so that you may refer to it as you go from one area to the next. For the most part, single hooks in areas that are non-buoyant lure restricted are standard, so, when

I refer to hooks, "Octopus" is the style I will be talking about.

There are many types of hooks, but it's the Gamakatsu Octopus style size two that I like to use most. It's strong, very sharp, and has always been 100% reliable, not to mention aesthetically pleasing to steelhead. I will say this over and over so you will understand my point. You get what you pay for! If you go with a cheaper hook, you will get fewer results. Years ago, in my efforts to save a little money, I went to a lesser-grade hook thinking that the only difference was the price. I took the hooks out into the field and lost each and every fish that I had on. The line didn't break, and the swivels didn't give it was the hooks themselves that actually broke. They broke in half. In all of the years that I had been steelheading I had never lost a fish, and on that horrible day I lost four of them. Not only had I lost the money from a lesser-quality hook but also I lost time and effort. I lost gas

money and all of the other expenses that come with a fishing trip, but the worst part for me was not having anything to show for my efforts. Believe me when I say learn from your mistakes. Gamakatsu is not the most expensive hook out there, but it is one of the most reliable. Now and again I lose a fish, but at least I'm not losing them to broken hooks.

Recycled Hooks

Just like everyone, I do all that I can to save money, and that means saving my hooks. I try to use them two or three times. Having the egg-loop on my hook

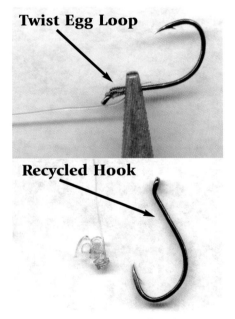

Twist Egg Loop

Recycled Hook

made that difficult until I found a way to get the line off without damaging the hook. Take a pair of needle-nose pliers and twist the line that is on the "shank" until you hear a pop. Remove the freed-up line and store the hook for later use.

Corkie (All Sizes and Colors)

There are several different sizes of corkies. They range from sizes 14 (the smallest) to size 6 (the largest). When you decide to fish with corkies you have to decide what

species of fish you are going after. The general school of thought is, the bigger the corkie the bigger the fish. I want to focus on sizes 14, 12, and 10. These are the optimal sizes for steelhead but don't be surprised if some other species decides to pick them up. These three sizes are dependent on water clarity, speed, and depth, as well as barometric pressure. You will need to cross-reference these variables all of the time as no two days, systems, depths or speeds of currents are ever the same.

In a high-pressure system with clear water, you are better off using a size 14, as the fish are very skittish for the most obvious reasons. A smaller-sized corkie and hook will not frighten a steelhead, though he may be more wary than normal. The corkie should be shiny and attractive. On days like this one you don't really need to use yarn, but if you decide to, it should be as small as you can get it. Scent on both the yarn and corkie is a good idea.

Size 12 is a nice well-rounded size for many occasions. You can fish a high-pressure system with this size, especially if the water is green. Green is one of the best colors of water to fish. With your polarized glasses you can see a lot more of what is going on even if you cannot see fish. You will be able to see places where the fish like to hold, even on bright sunny days. It's optimal to use scents and yarn to accompany your corkie. With green water,

fish are less spooked and on the look out for anything to pick up. This color of water predominantly follows rivers that have recently risen from rain and have just begun to recede.

For my needs a size 10 is the best all-around corkie. You can use it on a high or low-pressure system, though I would not recommend it if the water is gin clear. Pink, white, orange, and red are the best colors for this size. If one doesn't work right away, and you know for a fact that there are fish in the hold, then change your leader to a different color. I am implying that you have constructed all of your leaders at home and have put on various colors of corkie to accommodate the various weather and river conditions.

The corkie that you use should not interfere with the bite-area of the hook. If you place a corkie in the bend area of the hook, it should fit nicely inside it; if it does not, then your corkie is too big. If the corkie is too big you might as well be throwing out a weedless bass lure, because there is no way that any fish will be hooked reliably with your setup.

Every time that I go fishing and I am fortunate enough to get my leader back I take it home and scrutinize it very carefully to discern the difference, if any, between leaders that caught fish and those that didn't. I was doing this one day when I made a couple of very important discoveries.

In the photo below compare the leader hooks on the left with the ones on the right; the placement of the corkie is not the same. The one on the left is the same as any other leader I have used and caught fish.

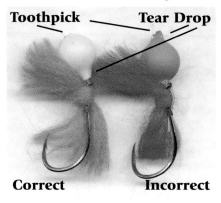

Toothpick ———— **Tear Drop**

Correct   **Incorrect**

Notice the toothpick that is jammed inside the corkie and you can see that the corkie has a teardrop shape at one end. Placement of the corkie has played a key role in many of the hits I have had. There are other variables as well, but this one is significant. I have done many experiments with this setup; most of them produce fish if I aim the teardrop towards the hook and the round end up towards the shank of the hook. Another thing to watch for is color chipping off the corkie, you should not recycle (re-use) a corkie that has a chip in it. Though you may not notice it right away, the fish will. The visual acuity of fish is remarkable. The tiniest deformity of the corkie will not go unnoticed by steelhead unless the water has absolutely zero visibility. If you pay attention to some of these smaller details, you will consistently catch fish more often than anyone you fish with who does not.

Cheaters

Cheaters let you get your presentation

higher without lengthening your leader. On occasion, you will need to use some of these for height issues without changing the weight or the length of the leader. Color still plays an important factor; also select them for size and then water clarity.

Toothpicks

I learned the value of toothpicks from a great teacher and I will always be indebted to him for showing me that I could increase the amount of successful hits to hookups just from this one little thing. After you have set your hooks and corkie to the leader, place one end of a toothpick into the top portion of the corkie and drive it down until it is snug between the

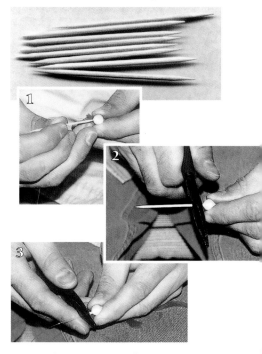

inside of the corkie and fishing line. Next, take your pliers and cut the toothpick as close to the corkie as you can without making it so short that you cannot pull the toothpick out with a pair of pliers at the end of the day. You will want to save as much of your gear as you can; hooks and corkies can be used time and again if given the proper care. Placing the toothpick in this manner will assure that the corkie will not go floating up your line, if that happens then you can bet that you will miss opportunities to set the hook when the big one hits your line nowhere near the hook. Though it seems like a small thing, use a round toothpick. I didn't think that it was all that important until a friend of mine asked if he should use a flat or round one. I told him that I had been using a round one but as long as he used something to keep the corkie stationary, it shouldn't make a difference. He had a box of flat ones, which he inserted into his corkies and promptly split all of them right down the middle. I highly suggest that you use the round ones.

Yarn

It's a good idea to have a variety of colored yarn. The yarn should complement the color of the hook and corkie. Sometimes I use a combination of colors just to change things up now and again, especially in areas that have a lot of pressure from fishermen. Twisting your yarn to the inside of the hook will ensure that if the fish goes after your yarn first, it will definitely hit the hook as well. You could also try tying your yarn so that it stays to the inside of your hook, which would be held in place by your egg-loop. I find that both are very good ideas. The only reason that I don't settle on the idea of tying the

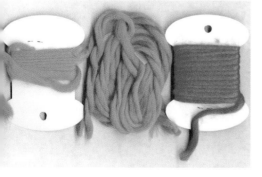

yarn directly to the inside is that the novice will have to cut his yarn very close to the point of hook as well as tying it and would run the risk of gouging his finger on the hook. The yarn is an excellent attractant and holds fish scent very well, which of course is another great reason for using it.

Pencil Lead

Though there are a number of other systems available, I have found that for almost all fishing needs this one works best. Pencil lead can be purchased rolled in various diameters. I use 1/8-inch pencil lead for most of my fishing needs.

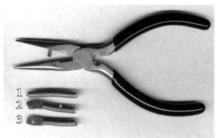

To prepare your lead, pinch one end of the clipped-off edge once or twice. Next, take your punch hole pliers and make a hole. Pencil lead will allow you to quickly decide how much weight you want to use in the field. Start with a longer piece of lead and snap the end off until the desired weight is achieved. The weight of the lead should not be so heavy that it drags on the bed of the river, rather, bounces every so often. It is diverse enough so you can decide how much lead you want to use in the field. I start out with large pieces and then progressively make them smaller. By starting out larger, I can use the same piece of lead for any river condition. If the water is deep and fast, use a heavier weight, and if it is shallow and slow use a smaller one. Sometimes the weight is so small that it doesn't look as though it performs any function at all, but be advised, it can

21

mean the difference between getting a fish and not getting one. The heaviest weight that you see in this section is 1/2-ounce, but each and every one gets down to the fish. The diversity of lead is based on it's ability to be modified quickly and easily. If you'rte using a light weight and don't want to change the weight, cast further upriver to get the weight down deeper in the river.

Slinky Weights

If you are going to fish water that has many boulders, slinkies are a very good idea. The slinky will allow you to slide over rocks that might be too close to each other. Pencil lead will get pinched and stuck between the cracks. If your weights get stuck, you'll lose your entire leader set-up. Because of the parachute material that comes with the slinky system, your weights will slide over and around the rocks in the water. Though pencil lead is

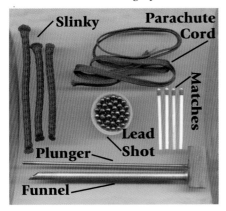

an excellent weight system, it is good to have a back up slinky system.

You can get the things you need to make slinky weights at your nearest sports store. Parachute cord is sold by the foot, and comes in standard or magnum sizes. Lead shot is sold in complementary sizes to the cord. Matches are needed to burn the excess ends of the slinky when you have achieved your desired size and length. The finished product will look

like the weight system you see in the picture at the bottom page of this page.

Cut the length of the cord that you want, paying attention to the fact that the longer your cord, the heavier your weight will be. Burn one end of the cord and pinch it tight with pliers. It should only take a couple of seconds for it to cool down enough for you to release it. Place the other end of your cord over a funnel. Place shot in the funnel and then force it into the cord with a plunger. Burn the other end of the cord as close to the shot as possible and then pinch it tight with the pliers.

You will lose fewer leaders over boulders than you would with pencil lead. Not losing your leaders translates into more time fishing and that means more hookups.

Tying Weights and Swivels Together

The swivels tie the mainline and leader together.

Most fishermen use a single snap swivel for the weight, leader, and mainline, but I use two. I know that over time, the movement of the swivel over either the mainline or the leader will cause abrasion. I have seen many fishermen successfully land a fish with that kind of terminal setup, but at the same time, I have seen many lose the fish right at the connection of the swivel to the leader. The reason they lost the fish was because of the abrasion that can occur. By using two swivels at that vital connection I know

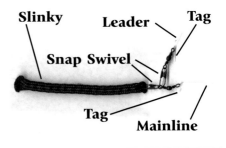

that if my line breaks it will not be because of the line or swivel interactions.

Though the illustration shows a slinky, you can use the same swivel setup for pencil lead. I use lead when I am drifting water that has smaller rocks, sand, or mud.

Swivels

The kind of swivel that you will need is a snap swivel. I like sizes 10 or 12; for the

most part they cover the widest range of needs. The premise is to keep your leader and weight system from tangling and preventing your line from twisting. The swivels are very strong, so don't let their diminutive size fool you. The only way that you can lose a fish due to a snap swivel is if you don't close it completely.

Clippers and Scissors

Clippers are a good all-around tool. They can cut just about anything that needs to be cut in the field, with the exception of lead.

Scissors allow you the quick freedom

to trim your line and yarn, but restricts you from clipping your toothpick or anything else that might be too difficult to cut with scissors.

Needlenose pliers

The pliers allow you to cut your lead and anything else that does not require a particularly sharp edge; they do not however cut yarn. You will need them for trimming your lead and pulling out hooks.

Lighter

The lighter is a tool you might never need in the field, but I take one along just in case. You might need to make a fire, or you might run out of pre-made slinky material. A lighter is small and convenient and doesn't weigh much, so it's worth bringing just in case you need it.

Beads

The primary function of beads is to protect your line from a moving lure above your hook and weights above your terminal gear. If you decide that your weight system should slide, then include a bead between the swivel and weight. Place a bead between your corkie and hook to protect your line from the impact of your corkie and the eye of the hook. The constant rubbing of the bottom of your corkie will cause wear and tear on the line, making it weaker until there comes a time that it can no longer take the pressure and will break. The purpose of the bead is to ensure that if the line does break, it's from fighting a fish and not because a corkie wore it down just enough for a fish or snag to break it.

When you use beads, consider their size. The size will have an impact on the weight of the leader, the larger the bead the heavier it will be, causing buoyancy to be sacrificed.

Vest

Choosing an appropriate vest for your needs is important. If you're going to do a lot of walking you might want to consider a vest with only a few pockets so you won't overload yourself. A vest with

many pockets tends to make us want to fill them. Think about the things that you need, and look for a suitable vest.

A vest should hold all of the essential equipment you will need. It should be light and durable, as well as organized. Whatever you decide to carry should be

easily retrieved from the pockets. Before leaving home, put your vest together as though you were about to go on a trip, then memorize the contents of each pocket. Put the vest on and try to locate something you would not ordinarily think about without looking at the pockets. I like to divide my vest into sections that are consistent with each other, tools with tools and hooks with hooks, etc. Knowing where everything is will save a significant amount of time in the field.

Fish Scents

The human body has an odor that fish will avoid, especially sweat. Our odors

transfer to everything that we touch. Monofilament line is very good at absorbing all kinds of odors and scents. Knowing this is the key to getting more fish to bite your hook. One of the last things you should do just before you cast out into the water is put some artificial scent oil on your offering, and slide it up and down your leader. The scent will disguise your body odors and let the fish concentrate on the more desirable scent. Sometimes the only difference between getting a fish to bite your hook and not getting a bite at all is the scent that you put onto your line.

Many sports stores have a wide variety of scents. Use the scent that is appropriate for the species of fish that you are going after. A scent that is attractive to a bass is not always attractive to a salmon or steelhead. The packages in the stores will help you make your decision. For steelhead I recommend shrimp oil, salmon milt, salmon egg, or crayfish scents.

Just before I go fishing, I take the scent out of its original package so no one will be able to tell what I am using. The reason I do that is so I can change the scent when fish are pressured without tipping off other fishermen as to what I'm doing. It's true; sometimes the only thing that turns off fish is the scent. So, bearing that in mind, when I go to a river with a lot of fishermen, I try to find out what the most-used scent is and make sure not to use it.

Of the concoctions you see in the picture on page 24, most of them are of my own design. One of the best scents I have ever come across was combining a gel and liquid scent together. I like to make combinations of shrimp oil with shrimp gel. Experimentation is a great way to find out what the fish want.

Worm Scent

Sometimes a good alternative is needed to catch fish that have been heavily pressured. Nowadays you don't have to go out and get some worms, you can get a scent with a worm odor. Some fishermen fish with worms and nothing else and they produce fish. You drift them the exact same way you do anything else. Sometimes you have to go back to the basics, at times the basics are the best things to put into the water.

Bait, Shrimp, and Egg Scent

The battle over which is the best bait and scent is a seemingly endless one. I have seen both work, but almost never at the same time. When I refer to either shrimp or eggs, I am referring to scents as well. There are many fishermen who prefer eggs to shrimp and would never consider using anything else. Eggs work very well, but they do not always produce fish. Shrimp have the same problems and successes as eggs. It is wise to go into the field with both. There are those who use shrimp and eggs on the same hook, and they get hookups, but their presentations are absolutely huge. I would not recommend this combination in clear water just because it is so large. If you opt for one or the other, it is best to have a backup of the opposite choice.

Thermometers

Knowing the water temperature will help you to understand the metabolic state of the fish. If the temperature is warmer, use a smaller offering because the fish are very active; if the temperature is colder, the fish will be more lethargic and less inclined to hit your lure so use something that offers a larger profile (presentation). A thermometer really helps you figure out what to use. If the water is 32 degrees or colder and the water is gin clear, use a shorter leader and your offering will need to have a greater profile. This is just about the same thing that you would do if the water were warmer and with zero visibility. Do the exact opposite if the water is 42 degrees and gin clear. Lengthening your leader and using a smaller offering is the best approach for the same conditions.

Knives

Always bring a good sharp knife for preparing your fish for the trip home. You'll need to clean the fish to preserve

the quality of the meat. The size of the knife should be based on the size of the fish. If you use a knife that is too small, you could accidentally cut yourself when you fillet your fish.

Stringer

The primary function of a stringer is to retain fish. What that means is, you do not string up a fish and then release it after it has had its gills damaged by the stringer. A fish that is placed back into the water after having its gills traumatized will die from the shock. The regulation handbook reads: "Once you have retained your daily limit you can no longer fish." You do not keep fishing with fish on the stringer in the hopes of catching a bigger and better fish. If you are near your limit think about what you want to do. You can catch and release fish if you don't keep that last fish.

Another reason to have a stringer is that you keep your fish extremely fresh if you keep them alive. If you prepare your fish for transport just before you leave, it will be very fresh when you get it home for either consumption or storage.

File

No matter how sharp you think your hook might be, it will always become dull with use. To touch it up, you'll need a small hook file. Let's say that the hook is in your left hand and the file is in your

Stroke

right: Lightly stroke the hook in an upward motion in the same direction as the tip (tine) of your hook. The first few times you do this you will only need to stroke it a couple of times, but as time goes by you will need to do it more. When you have to stroke your hook more than ten times it is time to change hooks. The cost of a hook is minimal, so don't worry too much if you need to replace a few of them while you are in the field.

Flashlights

Flashlights are a necessity for night fishing. As you purchase your flashlight, consider that your hands need to be free for tying knots and tying on your leader, not to mention that your arms will probably

be full when you are walking down a trail at three o'clock in the morning. There are many styles of flashlights available in sporting goods stores. Wearing a head-lamp is a definite plus for keeping your hands free. There are flashlights that you can clip to your clothing, and snake-lamps that you can manipulate. You can get most of these in any hardware store, and you'll pay less than what you would pay in a sporting goods store.

Camera

A camera can be worth its weight in gold. A visual documentation will help you to understand barometric pressure, time of day, weather conditions, temperature, water clarity, water visibility, water cur-

rent, relative water speed, and documen-tation of the fish caught. It is a "must-have" record that cannot be disputed. It also allows you to catch and release with a good conscience. If the only reason you want to keep your record-size fish is to show others that you did in fact catch a record fish, you have the option not to kill it. You can take dimensional photos and have a replica made. Putting a large fish back into the water will help to prop-agate the species with stronger genetic material, which in turn will make large fish available for future fishermen.

Screwdrivers

Screwdrivers are an essential part of your equipment. You will need a Philips and a

standard. It is a good idea to have main-tenance equipment in case you have to take apart your reel to get debris out. I rec-ommend that you only open your reel if it is an emergency because you run the risk of losing parts in the field.

Gear Oil

Now and again you will have to clean and lubricate your reel. Gear oil plays a vital part in making sure your reel lasts a life-time. Refer to your warranty and manual when you apply it to your reel. When you clean out your reel pay attention to whether or not the existing oil is dark; if it is, you need to clean it out and replace it accordingly. Bear in mind that some-times, less is more when you apply grease and oil to your reel.

Small Plastic Storage Bags

I do a lot to trim the amount of weight I carry into the field. Many of the items I carry are small and tedious; almost every-thing I carry needs to remain dry. Rather than carry small boxes for all of my small things, I pack them around in zip-lock storage bags. They are compact and light, while at the same time keeping every-thing dry. I always take back-up bags for accidents. Hooks can have a debilitating effect on these bags.

Tape Measure

The main reason to take a tape measure is to replace a weight scale. You can use a formula that is used by many fish hatch-eries to calculate official weights. Length x girth squared divided by 800 will give you a very good idea of how much a fish weighs. Be sure that you take any record-sized fish to a Fish and Wildlife

Department facility for an official documentation.

Following is an example of the calculation I just gave you. Above is a steelhead I caught in the Humptulips River. It was 37 inches long, and 20 inches around, so the calculation would go like this 37 x 20 x 20/800 = 18.5 pounds.

Gloves

Wool gloves have a variety of functions, but the one that no one talks about is the one thing you need to know most. Wool

gloves are great for helping you "tail" a slippery fish without hurting it. I am not a big fan of using nets because the only way for them to work is to pull the fish out of the water and damage their scales. By using wool gloves you stay warm during the fall and winter months, but you can protect the fish you just caught whether you are practicing catch and release or you want your fish to remain picture perfect for photographs.

Monofilament Fishing Line (Highly Visible vs. Invisible)

Fishing line is one of the most important things that you will have to think about prior to fishing. Not every line is suitable for every species of fish. In the case of steelhead, the criteria for the line is especially critical. All families of salmon are far more abundant than steelhead, regardless of what the fisheries department tells you about chinook (the hatchery run, not the native).

Often you will have to travel for no less than three hours to reach your fishing destination; travel is standard procedure. The last thing you want is to be out in the woods, miles from any store that sells fishing equipment, when your line breaks, or when you look in the trunk of your car and see that you didn't bring an extra spool of line. Precautions will ensure that you don't ever have to worry about that kind of thing happening. Always have an extra spool of line in the trunk of your car, or the back of your truck. The line should be sealed so odors will not adhere to the highly-absorbent monofilament.

I have developed a brand-new way to catch fish that goes against the grain of the vast majority of fishermen, but my research and practical application have proven that the method of fishing I am sharing with you is 100% reliable. The difference is in the line. I have broken the line down into two necessary categories.

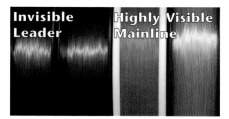

1) Your mainline is the line that comes directly off your reel that you tie to the swivel that will mark the end of your mainline and the beginning of your leader. Your mainline should be extremely "visible". I like to use X-T Solar 14 to 12-pound test for my mainline. It is strong and flexible under almost every condition. It is highly visible and resists abrasion. The visibility of the line will ensure that even if your leader is eight feet long you will be able to actually "see" your line give tell-tale signs that a fish is touching the end of it whether you feel it or not. You can reference what I am

telling you with the casting portion of the book. And 2) Your leader should be the exact opposite of your mainline. It should be "invisible". This is the portion of your line that you tie to the swivel from your mainline and goes to the hook or hooks directly (the leaders should be made in advance so that all you have to do in the field is tie a leader to your mainline with a snap swivel. It will save you an immense amount of time so you can spend more time fishing). It should be at least two pounds lighter in test than your mainline so if you get hung up on structure the only things you will lose is either your leader or weight. I use Maxima Ultra Green. I don't buy the leader packages that are in the sporting goods stores; the spools they sell for mainline are just as good as the leader packages and are much cheaper. Remember, you get what you pay for, and nickels and dimes add up fast.

Leader Holders

These are vital for transporting your leaders to the field. The leader holder I use can be found in any hardware store, called plumbing insulation. The insulation is cheap and easy to cut to any size that suits your needs. It is ideal for holding leaders because it is soft and will not cause line abrasion when you place your leaders on them.

The process of making your leaders should be done at home. Making them in the comfort of your home will ensure that you spend more time fishing. Someone once told me that he never went down to the river with a leader made in advance. He told me he would rather spend his time fishing over anything else. I asked him if he was spending all of his time at the river tying leaders how much time was he actually enjoying fishing? He understood the flaw in what he was saying and quietly walked away. I wasn't trying to cause a problem, but I really wanted to

know if he knew something I didn't. If it takes you three minutes at home to prepare a leader that is ready to put in the water, how much more time do you think it will take in the field? Based on the fact you will be standing and all the tools you will need will have to be spread out before you on the ground, you could easily add another minute or two to each one of your leaders. To make things even more complicated you might end up having to make a couple dozen leaders. It easily translates into over an hour in the field doing something other than fishing. How much enjoyment could you possibly derive from that? In your house, watching your favorite television show is a great time to make leaders. Use plenty of common sense and you will be more productive.

Hip and Chest Waders

When I talk about boots I am referring to neoprene waders or hip wader boots. Each pair you buy should be one or two

sizes bigger than your ordinary foot size. Make sure that the boots you are wearing have plenty of give and you will be far and away more comfortable than someone who didn't. During the colder months you will want to wear warm socks. If the boots that you are wearing are too snug you could cut off the circulation to your feet and they will get cold very fast.

The bottom of your boots should reflect the kind of fishing that you want to

do. If you are going to be in the river, you want felt on the soles of your boots, and if you are going to fish along the bank you want to go without felt. Felt becomes very slippery in mud and will cause you to trip and fall. If you have to do a lot of walking and you intend to fish "in" the river be sure to take extra precautions around mud puddles or your rear-end could become intimately acquainted with the ground. If you intend to stand in the river to fish you will definitely want felt.

On the left is a standard pair of boots with felt bottoms that fit over neoprene waders. They afford me the ability to walk on rocks that are covered in moss and algae. The waders on the right were used because the water I needed to be in was not too deep and the gravel bar that I am standing on tells you that there is not a slippery surface. Since I was going to stay to the edge of the water I opted for hip-waders.

Felt will help your feet hold firm to the algae that has grown on the rocks in the water.

Plain-soled boots are just as slippery in the river as are felt-soled boots in mud. The difference between the two is that slippery boots in the water can be extremely dangerous. If you fell in the wrong place you could be swept down stream. Use caution when selecting your boots and think about what you will be doing for the day.

Hats and Polarized Glasses

Whatever kind of polarized glasses you opt to buy, be sure that a brimmed hat accompanies them. Light rays that penetrate the tops and sides of your glasses will interfere with the function of taking the glare off of the water. If you want to see how ineffective glasses can be without the hat, try an experiment. Go to your nearest fish hatchery and look into the pools of water that are holding fish with your glasses on without a hat. After you have looked for a while, cup your hands over the sides and tops of the glasses and then look into the same area that you were looking and notice the vast improvement in water clarity and your ability to spot fish. Even on a bright, sunny day you will want to use your glasses and hat because you could miss out on spotting fish due to glare.

Raingear

Remember what I have told you, you get what you pay for. In the case of raingear, this is particularly true. If you only want to spend a couple of dollars for your protection, then you will only get a couple dollars worth of protection. Most cheap raingear will fall apart and fail you very soon after you buy it, however, the raingear you want does not have to be expensive. It should protect you from the elements, while allowing your body to breathe in the heaviest downpour. It should fit loosely over your body. Many products out there now have a technology that is excellent in almost any condition; Micromesh-fiber is the way to go. Many companies offer it, but you can bet that it won't be cheap; however the products will last for years. You get a lot of wear out of them and as long as you pay attention to the care instructions, they will last for years. Weather should not keep you from fishing; I suggest that if it does then you don't have the right raingear. There is no reason for you not to enjoy steelheading in any weather condition. Though my camera is wet, my compatriot and I are bone dry. Just by looking at us, you would never know that it had rained incessantly throughout the day.

Regulation Handbook

It is imperative that you take along the regulation handbook that comes out each year. It is your insurance. It's not that you will need it all of the time, but there may come a moment that you will desperately want it. It is the dubious few who make it tough for the rest of us. If we make the Game Warden's job just a little easier then we can all have a better time fishing. Know the regulations for the area in which you are fishing! The law does not forgive ignorance. Pay attention to the changes that come each and every year. The criminals out there adapt to the laws and so the laws have to keep upgrading to protect wildlife and you. If a Game Warden ever asks you for a pen, you had better know that it is a trick to keep you honest. If you ever say that you don't have one he will know that you are fishing illegally and you can kiss your gear goodbye. Don't try to pull the wool over their eyes when they ask you why you are still fishing when you have retained your daily limit, they have heard it all, and you will be fined for continuing. Defend yourself, be a good citizen, and have the handbook with you at all times.

License

You see it many times when you go fishing, a Game Warden comes down to the riverside and some fishermen will leave as fast as they can without him seeing them. It is the job of the Game Warden to catch as many of those people as he can because they don't have a license. Fishing without the proper license is the same as poaching. The Game Warden is not the enemy. They take a dim view of anyone without a license, and ignorance is not an acceptable excuse to be fishing without one. It is up to you to know the rules and regulations of the water you are fishing. Most of the Game Wardens whom I have met are very amiable and kind, quite the opposite of those fishermen who don't have a license.

I was able to hook, fight, land and release this beautiful fish while staying dry, cool, and comfortable by prearranging my gear. Streamlining what you wear and the tackle you use will greatly benefit you in the field.

Setup Considerations

Drag

The drag is not something you should be trying to set while you are fighting a fish. The last thing you need is one more thing to worry about when you have a fish flailing about at the end of your line. The drag on your reel should be set long before you go into the field. A great way to set it is by setting up your rod at home as though you were tying up to go fishing. Tie your line to a scale and pull back on your pole until one third of the strength of your line reveals itself on the scale. That means if your line is ten-pound test then three pounds of pull is sufficient. By the time any fish can pull the rest of the line out of your reel it will be at the maximum of ten pounds. Remember: set the drag to 1/3 of its capabilities. This premise for setting your test is good for any reel at any test. If you need to stop the fish in a hurry you can also apply your thumb to the side of the spool very gently. If you do this, pay attention not to apply too much pressure or for very long or you risk the chance of snapping your line.

The Bite Area

Not many people discuss this crucial topic because not many people even know how important it is. When talking about drifting the corkie, you'll want to consider the size of the hook versus the size of the corkie. If you use a size-ten corkie you want to use a size-two hook, for a couple of reasons. The most obvious is the "bite area". By using the proper combination of

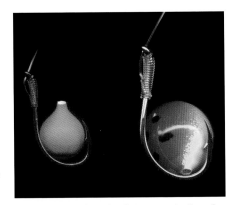

hook and corkie the bite area is free for hooking fish. That is, when the fish goes after the offering it will not only get the corkie, but the hook as well. To demonstrate my point, I found a leader that was left by some other fisherman in the field (see photo above). The size of the corkie on the right does not match the size of the hook. I am sure that he was looking for a large profile, but in doing so he interfered with the bite area. See how the corkie is too big for the hook when I place the two side by side? Because of this interference he would have never been able to hook a fish reliably: that translates into a fish that may have bitten into his offering, but was never hooked.

Now look at the hook with the pink corkie. See how the corkie fits nicely into the belly of the hook? This is a good rule to follow. If the corkie does not fit into the hook without interfering with the bite area, then the corkie is too big.

The next issue is buoyancy. If the corkie is too small, the weight of the hook could cause it to descend to the bottom of the river and never be seen by any fish, not to mention that it could easily get snagged on something. If you are going to use a size-two hook, then use the appropriate-sized corkie. A size-two hook will sink a size-fourteen corkie. If you still want to use a larger hook, but a smaller corkie, you could opt to double up (use two corkies) and counter the buoyancy issue. For presentation purposes, I recommend that you only double up for smaller setups, unless the water is muddy.

The Hook Setup

To the naked eye, this hook setup looks simple and standard with regard to drift-fishing equipment. It's the minute complexities that set this particular style of setup apart that have allowed me to catch many steelhead. To appreciate what is happening here, we have to dissect it.

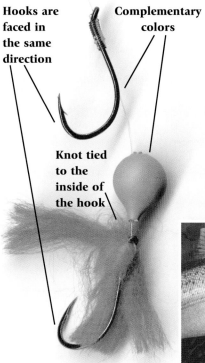

Hooks are faced in the same direction

Complementary colors

Knot tied to the inside of the hook

You first need to make the decision whether or not you want the fish to see what you are presenting. The hook style and color are important. Though hooks now come in many colors, there are some that will seem to disappear to fish. Black, silver, nickel, or gold are the colors of choice to hide any hook. They blend in well with almost any environment you will find in water, they are all natural colors. Just consider for the moment that you are a fish and you see one of these hooks coming at you. You're going to focus on whatever the hook is attached to, rather than the hook itself because you can't see the hook. By taking an unnatural object and applying the same color of hook to it you can hide the hook by making it appear as though it were part of the body of the lure. By giving it more volume and magnifying its bite area around the hook, you increase the possibility of getting more fish hookups. Since the fish of your choice thinks that the hook is part of the natural "presentation," it will readily go after your hook as well as the rest of the lure. By narrowing the focus of the fish's attention to the presentation of the entire hook setup without diverting it away from the hooks, you increase your chances of more successful strikes.

When drift fishing, I consider the hook color along with the color of the corkie. Predominately, I prefer cerise pink so I use the color of hook that will complement the corkie; I use a size-two

octopus Gamakatsu red hook. Look at the placement of the hooks on page 35. I place them facing the same direction to minimize the profile, thus increasing the bite area. Though it may sound redundant, I want the fish's focus to be as narrow as possible so that when the strike comes it will enhance my chances of setting the hook the first time the fish takes the lure. By narrowing the focus of the fish's intention I ensure that I will not miss a strike. If I were to widen it, that is to say, if I were to aim the hooks in the opposite direction of each other, I would enhance my chances of missing a hit because the fish's focus would be too wide, allowing it's attention to be less streamlined.

Though it is a double-hook rig, neither the second nor the first function as trailer hooks. Both of the hooks behave the way a primary hook would if it did not have a trailer hook. I have placed the corkie between the two so a few things can be accomplished. The placement of the corkie and toothpick assures me that when the fish strikes it will not be striking at the corkie two or three feet from the hook. The toothpick and first hook prevent it from floating up the line when I am trying to make a more natural presentation. With the placement of the toothpick sometimes you will get a strike as soon as your setup hits the water. If you set up any other way you will never feel the strike, let alone know that you even had one on at the beginning of the drift. The next reason for the setup is to make the whole thing appear to be one solid object as opposed to three or four different parts. Again, the placement of the hooks assures me that no matter where the fish strikes, it will hit the hook. Many times the fish will strike the first hook instead of the second one.

I place a toothpick into the corkie next to the line. The placement of the toothpick assures that the corkie will not spin around and cause abrasion on the egg loop. Though it will only move a tiny bit when it is in the water without the hook, it will move enough to damage the line on the second hook without the toothpick. Common sense tells you what happens if you let it go too long: you will lose the bottom hook and corkie entirely, due to line abrasion.

There are two reasons to use yarn: the first reason is that yarn helps to tangle the sensitive teeth of steelhead. It gives you about two extra seconds to figure out that you have a fish on the end of your line. Most fishermen that go out every season to catch steelhead will tell you that two more seconds is a world of time. It's the edge you will need. The second use for yarn is to hold scent. Artificial scent is an important attractant, and a mask to hide the scent of humans. People emit pheromones through the skin that are offensive to fish. It comes off our hands to our lures and line. Monofilament is not quite a solid and not quite a liquid, but rather something in between, so fishing line (monofilament) is porous and holds smells that come in contact of it. Make sure you do all you can to avoid getting offensive scents on your line directly by not touching it with your bare hands. Also, do not store extra line near chemicals when you put them away for the season, the odor of the chemicals can transfer to your line. You might forget about smells and odors, but I guarantee the fish won't. The general olfactory sense of a fish is 5000 times more sensitive than a human's. One third of its brain is dedicated to that purpose alone. If you can imagine a smell so intense you could *see* it, you would begin to appreciate why scent is so important to a fish. It is a huge thing that must be overcome if you are to be successful.

Do not clean your hands once you have applied fish scents, as some fishermen would have you believe. Placing scent on your yarn will cause some residual scent to stick to your fingers. While scent is stuck to your fingers, slide it up and down the length of the leader—the added scent to the leader will aid in streamling a fishes strike: even then, you will still have some on your fingers. Don't wipe it off! You will need the fish scent on your hands each and every time you check your line or hook.

Checking your line or hook is something a good fisherman will do often. The yarn that is tied to the egg loop on the hook is also very important. Notice the placement of the yarn; it's tied to the inside of the hook. In their efforts to tie up fast, many fishermen overlook what they are doing. By placing the yarn on the outside where the egg loop is, they are in essence saying they want fewer hookups. Placing it on the outside is contrary to their rush to get their lines out into the water, it widens the strike area instead of streamlining it. No one wants to go through all of that trouble just to minimize the opportunity to catch a fish, but when you place your yarn on the outside that is what you are saying, in essence. What I do is tie up as everyone normally does, but then I twist the yarn to fall towards the inside of the hook. Follow this train of thought. If the yarn is what the fish is going after and it's sitting just above the inside of the hook, then it stands to reason that each fish that goes after the yarn will inevitably hit the hook, and you will get more fish on in the process. Because you are simply twisting the egg loop and yarn towards the hook, it can turn around towards the back of your hook, so check it often. If it does, just twist the line back to the inside and continue fishing. The length of the yarn should never go past the end of your hook. More often than not, fish will touch your yarn and discover that something is wrong. You can give yourself more opportunity for hookups if the yarn is right there at your hook point and not below the bend of the tine, so even if the fish does figure out that something is wrong it will be too late to do anything about it. It will be on your hook and the fight is on.

The line I use for my leader is Maxima Green. Your line is an extremely important part of the setup. For your leader, use the most invisible line you can find. It should be limp and strong at the same time. It should also allow for shock absorption when the fish strikes.

Your hook setup is important. Your chances of getting a fish on greatly increase if you follow each step that I have laid out. There is no halfway about it. If you skip a step, then your chances of hooking and landing a fish diminish.

Leaders

I have been fishing for a very long time. I know that every old-timer out there has his own opinion about how long a leader should be, but the issues of the leader are more complex than just the length. Questions such as, what kind of line should I use? What length of leader should I use for the varied water conditions? What strength of test should I use? There is no mystery about the answers to these questions, as the conditions out in the field will vary from person to person. Not everyone goes to the same place all of the time. The leader length and diameter is dependant mostly on water clarity, however there are other variables that can come into play that can dictate changing your leader length.

Standard leader length is based on water clarity. The clearer your water is, the longer your leader should be. If you are fishing an area that has had a lot of people pounding the water, and the water is pretty clear, you need a long leader. If you have a hundred men fishing in less than a hundred yards, most of the fish are going to be spooked by just about anything that you throw at them. They will be forced further out from shore and deeper than they normally would be. The only way to counter that kind of "pressure" is to present something that does not look like the rest of the offerings, and that means putting on a longer leader. If all the fish sees is whatever you are offering and not a lot of garbage behind it, such as your weights and swivels, then it will feel more inclined to strike your hook more so than anybody else's. It just makes sense that taking the pressure off the fish will give it something else to think about, like striking at your hook. That means sometimes your leader will have to be over six feet long. There are many fishermen who will take issue with a six-foot leader. They will tell you that if your leader is six feet long then it will take your terminal gear twelve feet to pass by the fish before you feel a hit. The math makes sense, but it is not true. The longer leader will almost always draw a strong hit. Remember, I said that it would almost always draw from the fish a strong hit. This technique applies to water that is heavily pounded. When there is not much pressure from many fishermen in one spot, the length of the leader changes. When there aren't many things being thrown in the water, fish relax and come closer to shore. Even with crystal-clear water, the length of your leader does not have to be more than four feet; I never let it get shorter than two feet.

When the pressure is off steelhead it becomes easier to know what it is they are looking for. Start out with a four-foot leader and keep making it smaller as the day progresses if you are not getting any hits. Always begin with a long leader because you can't make a short leader long, but you can make a long leader short. When you do this you are able to use the same leader at various lengths without having to make an entirely new leader each time you want to change leader length.

When the water is muddy, you want to shorten your leader. Two feet is the longest the leader should be, based on the visibility factor. Fish tend to go down towards the bottom of the riverbed in colored water so your hook will have to be right in front of their faces before they even know to strike at your corkie. Regulations permitting, you can have your leader as short as a foot. When the water is at zero visibility, the shorter your leader the better. As a consequence of the leader being so short, you will have a lot more time to set your hook.

Mainline

The mainline is the portion of line that takes most of the girth on the spool. It is usually heavier than your leader by a couple of pounds. The premise is that you will prefer to lose your leader as opposed to losing a large portion of your mainline when you are fighting a fish or if you are hung up on a snag. When setting your drag, set it to the strength of your leader and not the mainline. If you set your drag to the mainline and not your leader you will lose many more fish because your leader-line will snap routinely under the stress. Let's just say for the moment your mainline is twelve-pound test and your

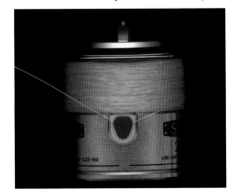

leader is eight-pound test, if your drag is set to the strength of twelve pounds you will lose the fish because the leader is eight pounds, which is 1/3 weaker.

Your line should also be abrasion resistant. It should resist nicks and cuts from the sub-structure of the water, such as, logjams, rocks, weeds, boulders, and occasionally lost line from other fishermen who have fished the same drift.

At times you will need to make adjustments in your fishing tactics. Rethinking the premise of your mainline should sometimes be a consideration. I have caught many fish on six-pound test. I'm not a masochist, so just hear me out.

The casting range of any rod is really based on the width of the line, and the line is based on test capabilities, and what we decide to use is based on our capabilities as fishermen. I have had occasion to cast out into a river as far as sixty or seventy yards. The only way I was able to do it was to reverse the size of my mainline and my leader, that is, I made my mainline six-pound test and my leader ten pounds. Sometimes the only way to get to the fish from shore is to cast out very far, and to do that you must accept a few things, you are going to lose a lot more leaders than usual because your mainline is much thinner than your leader. I came up with the idea when I found a river-system that had most of the fish on the other side; I was unable to get to the fish because it was too deep and fast to get across, and I didn't have a boat at the time. The fish were over there because the fishermen who had been there had pressured them into moving. I was going to leave the area and go somewhere else when I started thinking of the reasons why I was leaving. The reason I decided I had to leave was because I was unable to cast to the area that the fish had gravitated towards using convention methods. I thought that if I used have a smaller test,

then I would be able to get there, but that meant I would have to use an even lighter leader, and I was already using a six-pound leader, so I reversed the leader test and mainline to achieve the distance. Though I lost a lot of line and spent an inordinate amount of time tying line, I hooked into a lot of fish. Thinking outside the box and inside the parameters of the law allowed me to come up with an idea that made an un-fishable area produce fish. Fishing in this way should only be done once you have fully accepted the idea you are going to lose more leader and mainline than you normally would if you fished with a stronger mainline and weaker leader.

Tying Knots

Your line is only as strong as your weakest link, and sometimes that weakest link is your knot.

The clinch knot is one that a lot of bass fishermen use, but as far as I am concerned it is inappropriate for drift fishing. I have seen many fishermen lose their fish because they were using it. It broke the line and the fish swam away.

The improved clinch knot is another matter altogether. It has two loops as opposed to the one that is used in the original knot. This simple modification improves the strength of the kno dramatically, resulting in fewer fish lost.

Tying the Improved Clinch Knot

1. Place the hook in your left hand and the line in your right.

39

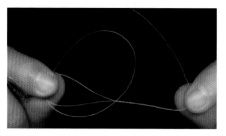

2. Guide the line through the eye of the swivel two times so that you end up with a loop and a long "tag" end.

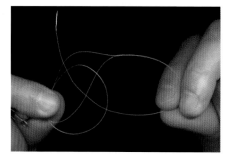

3. Wrap the tag end around the line six or seven times. Take the tag in your right hand and place the tip of it through the two loops in your left hand so the tag continues through until it is long enough to grab.

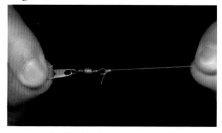

4. Next, hold the line in your right hand and pull the tag straight back so that it stays in direct alignment with the other end of the line, and tighten the knot. Clip the tag, and you are ready to fish. The clinch knot is also used to tie your terminal together.

Tying the Blood Knot

The blood knot is an excellent tool for tying two lines together, and is also used to tie "backing" to a tippet for fly fishermen. Sometimes when you get pounded by the big one that goes screaming down the river, the line on your spool diminishes to about halfway when suddenly the line breaks at the tip of your rod. Let's just say that your back-up reel has just about the same amount of line on its spool from your last trip and you didn't take the time to re-spool. The blood knot is an excellent tool for tying the two together. Like fly fishermen, you might want to consider using a stronger monofilament for the first 1/3 of the spool. It's a fine way to fill your spool with heavier test and still have enough light line to allow you to cast further out into the river. Bear in mind that it is not a necessity, but something to consider.

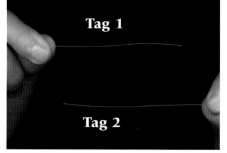

1. The first step involves using line of equal strength. Your tags should be no shorter than eight inches.

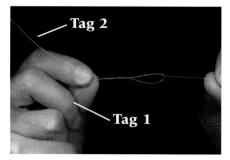

2. The two lines come together parallel. Take Tag One and wrap it around the other line six times, then take Tag One and direct it back to the starting point of the wraps. Place it between the two lines and hold it there.

Repeat the same process with Tag Two in the opposite direction of the wraps that were used in Tag One. If you started the wraps counter-clockwise with Tag One, then Tag Two should be clockwise.

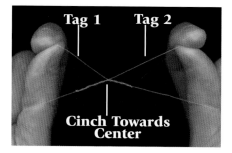

Tag 1   Tag 2

Cinch Towards Center

3. Now that the two tags have been brought to the center of the knot you are ready to start cinching the knot together. With your left hand holding both the end of Tag One and the starting point of Tag One, begin to pull Tag Two opposite of Tag One for a couple of inches. Take your time and go back and forth between the two tags a couple of inches at a time until the knot looks tight.

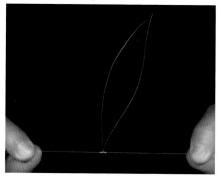

4. Trim both the tag ends and pull snug. Your blood knot is complete. Remember, even though it is a very good knot, it will not be as strong as the original line, so bear that in mind as you are fighting a fish.

5. The completed blood knot.

The Egg Loop

The egg loop is the vital connection to the entire leader setup, it holds your hook, yarn, and eggs. The following photographs are arranged so that you can match your hands to the pictures for an easier understanding of how to tie the knot correctly. Your hands should be positioned the same way a mirror reflects your image when you look at it.

Tying the Egg Loop

1. Start with the hook in your left hand and your leader in your right. Your choice of leader length is your discretion. Guide the tag end of the line through the eye of the hook to the bottom of the shank. Hold both the hook and the tag end of the line with your left hand.

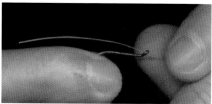

2. The line at the top of the hook should then be wrapped around the portion of the bottom of the eye going around it eight or nine times depending on the test of your line. Note: the smaller the test, the more times you will want to wrap around the hook.

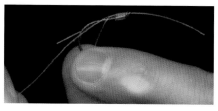

3. Place your wrapped line in your

right-hand index finger and thumb while holding onto the tine of your hook at the same time in the same hand. This will allow your left hand to be free so you can take the end of the line and feed it through the bottom portion of the eye, starting at the end of the "shank" area of the hook and going the exact opposite of the line as it went through the first step of tying the egg loop.

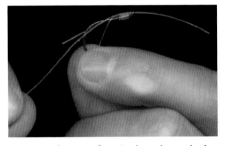

4. Insert three or four inches through the eye with the other end of the line while holding the hook at the bottom of it with your left index finger, forefinger, and thumb at the same time. Take the line in your right hand and wrap it around the hook shank six or seven more times immediately below the fist set of line-wraps.

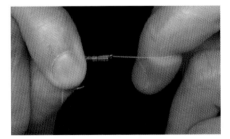

5. Take the line in your right hand and tuck it into the fingers of your left hand holding the hook, holding all of the line and hook together. Your right hand is free at this point to pull the tag end that is sticking out of the eye of your hook. Pull your line a little at a time through the eye, stopping now and again to make sure that the line in your left hand is not getting tangled, and continue to pull until

you can feel the line in your left hand tighten around your fingers.

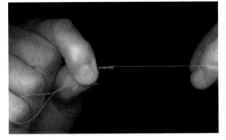

Give a small quick tug with your right hand and your egg loop will be complete.

6. The last step to the egg loop is to cut off the tag end of the line. Remember that the "tag" is the loose end that needs to be trimmed beneath the egg loop.

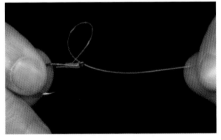

7. Finally, push back the line that extends out of the eye of the hook and you will make a loop for either eggs or yarn.

Tying on the yarn is important. When you do, make sure that the knot of the yarn is on the inside of the hook. Entertain for a moment that the knot of the yarn is on the backside of the shank of the hook. If the object of attention is the yarn and nothing else, then the fish will go straight for it, but bear in mind that fish are not perfect hunters. The fish may strike at the knot, but that does not mean that the strike will be straight enough for the mouth of the fish to engulf the yarn and hook at the same time. The fish may simply strike the lure or corkie with the very tip of its mouth and miss the hook entirely. By placing the yarn knot on the inside of the hook you are ensuring that no matter how subtle the strike is, the fish will bite into the hook whether it intends to or not. Something I like to do when the fish are lethargic is put a double-hook setup with the corkie in between the hooks. It is another way of taking the guesswork out of what the fish will or won't do.

There is another good reason to tie your egg loop in this fashion to the lines pulled through the lower portions of wrapped line in Step 5, the leader is straightened which diminishes line-twist. The lack of line-twist allows the corkie to flow more naturally during the drift and equates to more hookups.

As you remove your leader from the leader holder, pull on the line in the same fashion to further relieve line twist just before you cast out.

Line Abrasion

I have seen it time and again. In the efforts to get their hooks into the water many fishermen disregard the nicks in their lines. When drift fishing it is inevitable that you will get nicks in your line, I call that "line abrasion". The abrasions themselves are not the problem; it is the impatience of the fishermen that is the problem. If you have been stuck on a snag and you were lucky enough to get your leader back, then take a moment to stroke your leader with your fingers to see if there was any damage done to it. You could have line abrasion and not even see it. The tactile sense in your fingertips will tell you more than your eyes ever could. If you feel any nicks at all, change your line and you will be better for it and you won't end up hating your lack of self-control at the end of the day. Let's say you started out using ten-pound test and you get a nick in your leader. Well, instead of the ten-pound test that you started with, you could end up with six-pound test based on the nick in the middle of your leader. Change your leader at the first sign of abrasion and you will be rewarded for it in the end.

Look at the magnified line in the picture below. Pay attention to the lighter portions of the line. Those are nicks in the line. They are the weak points that will cost you a fish. The line is ten-pound test but the nicks make it weak to about six-pounds or less. What that means is if your drag is set for ten pounds and your weak point is six pounds, then your line is only as strong as the nick in your line and you will lose fish because you didn't check for these weak points. Whenever you find abrasions or nicks in your line, change it immediately. Stroking your line, with your fingers, now and again will ensure that you minimize chances of fish being lost.

Abrasions
(Magnified Line)

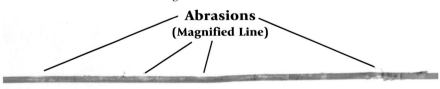

Reading Water

I often turn to science to help me understand what it is that fish need. It's not the fisherman's taste that catches the fish, but instead it's the fish's tastes that concern me. This is the very opposite of what others think about when they go into the deep dark woods in search of the perfect river that holds the largest and strongest fish they can imagine catching.

But for most, it is a pipe dream, because the truly gifted fishermen hold onto secrets that they will take to their graves. The competition, in their minds, is too great to let others know what they need to know in order to catch that once-in-a-lifetime fish, or for that matter, consistently catch fish at all. I am not of that mindset. I know the frustration of asking fishing guides questions that will not be answered.

I have read many different books on how to catch salmon and steelhead. It was a daunting task, but when I had finished what I found out was that almost everyone had an opinion on how to approach drift fishing, and almost all of them disagreed on how to go about tracking down and catching these elusive fish.

I sat down in my living room and thought about what to do next. I was staring at my goldfish, my face so close to the tank I could feel the coolness of the glass. I was thinking that all fish in some way or another must have some common predictable traits. It was then that I had an epiphany. It occurred to me that very few people ever talked about the scientific approach. You would be hard pressed to find a fisherman who didn't believe that

most of fishing was based on pure luck.

I waded through volumes of books, many of them contradicted each other. In the end I was able to ferret out some universal habits with regard to behaviors of salmon and steelhead. Many of the habits of fish are largely dependant on the water in which they reside.

The difficulty in understanding where to look for fish in various systems is an ongoing problem. "Reading" water is not as difficult as many old-timers would have you believe. I have personally talked to many very qualified fishermen who try to paint an air of mystique around fishing. I understand that some of them just want you to go out and earn your fish the same way they did. There is nothing wrong with that, but the fact that you go out to the stores and buy products that very often run into hundreds of dollars, and the time you spend investigating the sport, not to mention the time you take off from work, warrants that you have earned the right to all of the information they have. I want you to be able to read water just as easily as any of the old-timers so you can start reaping the benefits of your efforts right away.

Holding water comes in a wide variety of types but it's the ability to discern where the fish hold that will set you apart. Many times I have gone to fish water that was heavily pressured only to find myself in an area completely alone, while just a few hundred feet away were a bunch of guys in a small area. Just because there were a lot of men in one place did not mean that they were

Back Eddy **Seam** **Current** ⟶

Tailout

catching fish, at least not proportionate to the amount of men that were there.

I believe that if you study these pictures diligently you will know what to look for when you're on the river. All of these photos are bodies of water that will hold fish, and a brief description helps you understand what you are looking at.

Look at the water directly in front of the fishermen. There is a seam that runs parallel with the shoreline. The seam represents two distinct current flows. The darker portion (on the far side of the seam) is slower, and the lighter portion (the side closer to the fishermen) is faster. It is the slower portion of the seam where the fish lay in wait for food to come down from the faster portion of the river.

It's important to remember that you fish the seam before you do anything else. Just above the seam is a back-eddy. I was fortunate enough to have fished the seam around the back-eddy. I caught two steelhead in two casts. Of course it would be foolish to think that I could do this every time that I go fishing, but the fact remains that because I considered the scientific aspects of my environment (barometric pressure, precipitation, and wind) and cross-referenced them with the fish's environment (water height, flow, and clarity) I was able to land these fish

without investing an inordinate amount of time trying to find them.

Look at the science of drift fishing and you'll produce a tremendous amount of fish that you would otherwise not catch.

Back-Eddies

A back-eddy is typically formed when water flow passes an outcropping of land called a jetty. The swirling water forms a pool that is a great holding area for fish. This area of water flows in the opposite direction of the river. Because it is forced to go the opposite direction, the water in the back-eddy slows down. The seam of the back-eddy and the main current of the river is where you will find the fish.

In the above photo you can see me on a jetty fighting a fish that I had just hooked on the seam of a back-eddy. At the point of the rocks there is fast water. It's in the slow water just before the fast water that you will find the fish holding. The pool of water you see just below me is where you will find the more lethargic fish. That pool of water is a great place for plunking or bobber fishing. To find a back-eddy, remember: it is a portion of the river where water along the bank flows in the opposite direction of the main river.

Any time you see fast water pool up like this on the sides of the river you know that fish will be resting there before they continue upriver. The back-eddy, along the banks of the river, is an excellent place to locate fish.

Seams

Seams are found when two water currents meet, and where depth changes abruptly. In the photo you will see that the seam is further out and on a straight portion of the river. The young man above cast out and presented his size-12 corkie right through the seam from the fast water to the slow, his reward for such a perfectly

Pool   **Tailout**

natural presentation was this huge female. A natural presentation is extremely important.

In the photograph above, the red line shows exactly where the seam is. I will spend more time discussing this but the best way to read water is by rote. You have to look at many types of water before you will be comfortable, but it will come more easily if you take the time to look at these pictures as often as you can. Try to envision what the fish, facing into the current, might look like underneath the water. Invariably it will be waiting in the slower portion of the seam waiting for food to come down stream. It is equally important to consider what the fish are doing, besides waiting for a meal to come

downstream. They maintain their position hiding behind rocks and gravitating just above a tailout, or just below some fast water, called a "riffle".

In the photo below look across the river and find the water that slicks up and looks slow. The seam where the fast and slow water meet is where you want to cast your line. Because the water is both fast and slow, your options for fishing styles can be wide. For this particular scenario, you can plunk, drift, or use spinner baits.

Tailouts

A tailout is slower and slicker on the surface and occurs just before the water becomes very fast. It's where steelhead hold (rest) before they continue up river.

Can you see this tailout?

While there, they are on alert for any foods to help them regain their strength. This is a great place to fish.

Here's another tailout.

The photo below is another tailout. Along the edges of the tail (see red line)

of this stretch of water was a large school of steelhead. This body of water pooled from deep to shallow, and as you can see picked up speed once the water left the pool.

This is a classic tailout. The water pools deep, then shallows up, and then picks up speed again.

Under most circumstances, fish will hold at the extreme edge where the tail-out ends and the riffles begin.

The Riffles

The riffle (see photo at top of page 49) is the fastest portion of water located just below a tailout. It is the area where the fish are both preparing to move up the river and where they can rest. They will be looking for rocks and tailouts to rest in once they traverse the riffle. During a high-pressure system with clear water, fish gravitate to a riffle for cover. If you are able to see most of the riverbed, a riffle is a good place to start fishing. The refractive quality of the choppy water provided by the riffle is ideal for fish to hold during bright sunny days. Another area that fish like to hold in is rather surprising. During the fall months many of the rivers get flooded and muddy, "blown-out". To the novice fisherman it looks as though the water is un-fishable. Nothing could be

further from the truth. Because the water is moving so fast when flooding occurs, fish are forced to hug the bank.

I recall once when I was fishing some water that had recently been flooded. I was standing in a shallow, muddy portion of the river when I felt something bumping into my leg. I was concentrating so hard on what I was doing, I dismissed the bumping as a small branch hitting me because of the water being high, but what I hadn't noticed was that the bumping was in the wrong direction. The water was flowing from my left to right and it was my right leg that was being bumped. The fish bumped into my leg five times before I reached into the water just in time to feel an enormous tail swimming away from me. I got out of the water and started flipping my tackle out a couple of feet from the bank. In no time at all I had a fish on shore and that was how I spent the rest of my day; it was like fishing in a bucket.

Slots

This hold in the photo below, is called a "slot". You can see the water runs a little faster in the center of the slot and the sides are slick. It's the water that's running fast that is holding fish in this case. Though the water wass murky, I found a large school of steelhead in it. I stayed for most of the day catching many of them. Because visibility was zero, I was able to fish there without pressuring the fish out. Historically, when water is colored and murky it is a great time to fish without the threat of putting fish off the bite.

The picture above shows a body of water that deepens the closer it gets to the log. This is another slot, and an excellent hold for fish. Because the water is so clear, you need to sneak up on it from downriver and then drift from some cover. When the fish are running they will definitely hold here. Bear in mind, when you fish narrow and clear water you must slowly approach holds that have fish. Sudden movements cause shadows and images to get the attention of any nearby fish and they will be put off the bite.

The water in the photo below might be a little confusing. The large cluster of boulders sticking out into the water is called a "jetty". Just downriver from it, the water circulates into a back-eddy. Closer to the bottom of the picture you see that the water is split into two slots. Both sides of the slots will hold fish because they both slow down and deepen into pools. On the other side of the jetty is a pool that held a large school of steelhead, coho, and chum. I consider this to be a very productive place to catch fish.

Occasionally you might see a fish jump out of the water in the slower current. Many fishermen succumb to that sight and cast out at the fish that are jumping, only to drift water that does not produce consistently. The fish that are interested in striking anything are in the water that is a little riffled on the surface.

The water in the above photo is deep and not that fast. Based on the surface of the water, you can tell that the riffle is deeper and only slightly faster. It disturbs the water surface just enough to allow the fish there to feel less pressure because they cannot see you and you cannot see them. I guarantee that if you see fish in the water, they have seen you long before that and are on high alert. The stress they feel from your presence will keep them occupied enough so that they will not be interested in your offering.

Here the water is clear and you can see to the riverbed. The boulders house fish in front of and behind them. The water is slow and deep. You can plunk in water like this, or you can use spoons to entice a fish to strike. You also have a the third option of drifting further out into

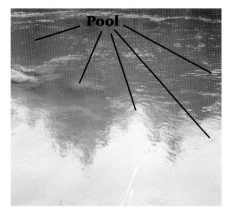

the river if the first two do not produce for you in a short period of time. Bear in mind that when the water is this clear, you need to approach it slowly and cautiously if you don't want to spook any fish. This shade of green is just the shade you are looking for. The water is clear, but not so much so that it puts off the fish from striking your corkie, lure, or eggs.

Experiment

Most of the time when you got to a river you will not be able to see the bed due to limited visibility. As you look at the water ask yourself if you know for a fact what kind of substructure is there. If you don't know, there is an experiment that will help you to identify boulders in dark water without the need to actually see them. Boulders provide excellent cover and holds for all anadramous species which is why you should perform this experiment. Take a large rock and place it in shallow water just deep enough to cover the rock. Study the affects of the water surface as it races over the top of it. It is a universal constant that all water will behave the same. If you can locate rocks large enough for steelhead to hide behind or sit in front of, you will catch fish. As I have said, fishing takes practice. You don't have to be patient, you just have to be determined to learn your craft.

Drifting Styles of Fishing

Drifting Spinner Baits
Modified to Hold Scent

The photo of the lure on the right shows a Vibrax number three single-point hook. For scent-holding purposes, I have tied yarn to it. The premise is that the fish should strike directly at the point of the hook. To prevent it from striking at the outside of the hook, which is true in most cases where yarn is tied to the outside, I tie it to the inside, thus diminishing the possibility of missing a hit from the fish. The knot that I used was an egg loop.

Clip the tags close to the body of the hook at both ends. The way the loop is tied will ensure that you will not lose the yarn. The first portion of the loop is the same as any egg loop, but you only add the yarn for the last portion so you can prevent tangles in the yarn when you go to cinch the line.

The presentation of the lure is the very same approach I use for drift fishing. Cast upriver to ten or two o'clock and let the lure fall until you think the lure is just above the bed of the river, then reel in the slack. The slower the water is, the faster your retrieval will have to be. Any fish that hits a lure like this will pound it so hard you will know the second it does.

This is an alternative to bobber fishing. In dead-calm water you can fish for steelhead as though you were fishing for any other kind of trout, and not interfere with the structure underneath. You should not have any problems with snags that are deep. The barrel swivel and snap swivel will counter-spin to make sure that no tangling of the line occurs. Water that

has been heavily "bobber" and "drift" fished should provide a nice alternative to the fish as they should be properly motivated to hit the lure even in the presence of strong pressure. This alternative should work in any slow to near stopped water.

Flipping for Steelhead
with Drift Gear

In the photo at at the top of the next column, I am pressed hard against brush, trees, and rocks. Based on the location, I could see that it was a nice back-eddy. It looked like a place that most fishermen would pass up, so I was confident the fish would not feel any pressure. The only problem was that I was going to have to modify my technique to get at the fish. I still intended to drift, but I needed to change my cast in order to get to them.

Flip casting is just what it sounds like. Instead of over-the-shoulder casting, you cast with your right hand, starting from your left shoulder, casting to your right. It's a backward cast that is good for close-

quarters fishing. If you are in an area full of brush you can fish it if you use the flipping technique. My modification of flipping involves casting directly into the current and reeling in the slack, as your line gets closer to you. By doing this, you have the weight coming before the corkie rather than vice versa; thus, the moment a fish touches your hook you will feel it each and every time, eliminating the need to watch your line at all times. Your drift gear becomes as sensitive as spinning bait, spoons, and jigs. Remember that you need to constantly reel in just enough slack to keep the weight off the bottom of the river so that the only thing you feel is

the touch of the fish as it hits your hook.

Flipping can be done in just about any tight area you might encounter. This technique opens up a lot of fishing areas you might not have entertained in the past. Below is an area I had been fishing using the flip technique. I was standing on an outcropping and had to walk along the bank until it was shallow enough for me to get into the water and tail the fish so that I could release it.

The overhanging branches and the deep pool formed by the back-eddy made it a perfect place for fish to hold, and to discourage other fishermen at the same time.

Gliding

Gliding is one of the best ways to be sure that whatever disturbs your line during a drift is a fish.

Step 1: If the river is flowing from right to left, to "glide" your gear you will need to cast out to about two o'clock. Without reeling in the slack, let it fall until you feel your weight hit the bottom.

Step 2: When it does, lift your rod about a foot, if the river is running at three feet or more. As your line goes through the drift be constantly aware of the slack and reel it in, as it gets closer to you. A belly in the line could cost you reaction time that would allow the fish to shake a hook loose that has not been properly set.

Step 3: As the line drifts directly in front of you at twelve o'clock, stop reeling. If at any time you see that your line slows down or stops, pull back on your rod and set the hook. Many times it will be a fish that is mouthing your hook and is simply moving it out of the way.

It may take you a few casts to familiarize yourself with the structure under the surface. When you are gliding, feel the weight of your line on your index finger and attempt to discern whether or not the line becomes a little heavier than normal; this is a dead give-away that a fish is on the end of your line. If you find that your weight is on the bottom more often than not, even though you are constantly reeling in the slack, lighten the amount of the weight and cast out again. When you are using a lighter weight and you want your leader to go deep, cast further up stream and let your line fall longer before you start to reel in the slack.

Plunking

High, slow, muddy water is designed for plunking (see photo on page 55). It is done with heavy terminal gear that cannot be drifted with typical gear because the water flows much too slowly for anything else. Deep pools and large slow back-eddies are areas designed for plunking. The weight you use is much heavier and the fishing tactic is not active.

The typical setup includes a mainline, three-way swivel, and a dropper line. The best time to plunk is during high, muddy water: that being the case, your leader can be just as thick and bright as your mainline would be if you were drift fishing.

Step 1: The mainline is tied to the three-way swivel.

Step 2: The middle portion of the swivel holds your leader offering, be it #4 Vibrax spinner, #8 spinning cheater or eggs. Because you want to use lures that spin, do not use a double-hook setup. To counter line abrasion, beads will replace the toothpick. The bead is placed between the rig and hook, rather than above it.

Plunking Rig

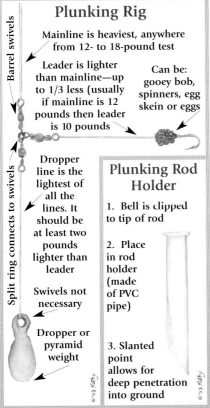

Barrel swivels

Mainline is heaviest, anywhere from 12- to 18-pound test

Leader is lighter than mainline—up to 1/3 less (usually if mainline is 12 pounds then leader is 10 pounds)

Can be: gooey bob, spinners, egg skein or eggs

Dropper line is the lightest of all the lines. It should be at least two pounds lighter than leader

Swivels not necessary

Split ring connects to swivels

Dropper or pyramid weight

Plunking Rod Holder

1. Bell is clipped to tip of rod

2. Place in rod holder (made of PVC pipe)

3. Slanted point allows for deep penetration into ground

Step 3: The dropper line is tied to the bottom of the swivel. It should not exceed twenty inches, but not shorter than a foot. The weight that it is tied to will be no less than two ounces, and less than five. There are many styles of weights to choose from, but the pyramid is the most widely used.

Step 4: Rod holders are used, along with bells that indicate when a fish is on.

Cast a short way out into a pool and let your gear fall until it reaches bottom. Reel in the slack until only the very tip of your rod remains slightly bent. Place the rod into the rod holder and attach the bell. When the bell rings set the hook.

The Premise of Bottom Bouncing

The only time I bottom bounce is on water that has boulders instead of gravel or a sandy bed. I find it is very difficult to tell when a fish hits my line while I'm bottom bouncing. There are measures you can take to minimize the negative effects of slack and tight line that is formed from bouncing along the bed of

the river. Cast up stream and let your heavy weight bounce along the bottom until a fish picks up the end of your leader. The problem of not feeling the fish take my line can be somewhat alleviated by using pencil lead, and bouncing lead-balls; however more often than not, for better sensitivity I like to use a slinky.

A slinky is a weight system that is comprised of parachute cord and lead shot of various sizes. It slides more than bounces over boulders, and will not grab onto rocks like pencil lead. It is still difficult to feel the hit from a fish, but the slinky weight system merits consideration if you want to improve your chances of feeling the fish take your offering. Remember to keep your index finger on the line at the guide as it comes off the spool and you will feel the fish take your line, as well as see it. Keep in mind that reeling in the slack is just as important as it is with gliding. Soon after the cast, reel in just enough line so that the slack is gone as the line becomes parallel to your position at twelve o'clock, and drift the rest of

the water until after you pass the optimal drift of two o'clock.

You can continue the drift by drift-mending your line. Drift-mending your line is paying out your line in a fashion that allows the line to continue down the drift, parallel to the bank long after it has left the optimal point of two o'clock, by flipping the bail and leaving it in the open position for a natural presentation while you keep your index finger with the line as it continues to pay out. The problem with drift-mending is that it is a completely "natural" drift, and you lose the ability to discern any strike due to "line-belly".

Probing Water

Probing the river is a must when the fishing is difficult. Finding fish that will take your offering can be rough between runs. If you understand the water you are looking at, you should be able to ferret out a fish or two even in the most difficult of times. You might end up investing a good deal of the day before you get your fist bite, but it will come. I was probing the Humptulips when this big chinook

hit my line. I hadcovered about a quarter mile of the river before I found her. Probing is one of the easiest things to learn about drift fishing.

The casts you make will be based on water clarity. If the water is muddy with very little visibility, then you cast at about one-foot intervals. What this means is wherever your terminal gear hits the water, cast out one foot past that on your next drift. If the visibility is two feet, then you cast every two feet, and so on until you have covered the width of the river or the fishable area that you're in. I have never failed to produce a fish in water that was probed. When you find a place that is producing, stay there until the bite goes off and then move on.

When the water was running low and clear I was able to find a school of salmon holding in a riffle by probing this river.

The Process of Fishing

Wading with a Pole

If you are going into water you're unfamiliar with and don't have polarized glasses to see the bed of the river, or if you are in water that is muddy with zero visibility, then you'll want to get yourself a pole to probe with. This does not mean you have to go out and buy one, find a strong branch from the riverside. When you probe water above your knees, move slowly, one step at a time. This is the safest way to walk across any river. If you must cross a river to get to a good fishing hole and it looks safe, be sure to scan the river above you for large debris that could come down and sweep you away. If it sounds like I am trying to scare you, I'm not. There are many dangers crossing a river you may be unfamiliar with; you can never be too cautious.

There are a variety of poles that you can buy, but you will have to carry it with you the whole time you're at the river. A good strap on the pole will ensure that it never leaves your side.

Casting

The art of casting is a marriage of both hands and arms working together and separately at the same time. The placement of the reel depends on whether you are right- or left-handed. If you are right-handed, the handle on the reel should be placed on the left side so you can fight the fish properly with your right hand. If you are left-handed, the reel should be placed on the right side so that you can fight the fish with your left hand. The idea is that you reel with your less-dominant hand and arm so your stronger one can be used to fight the fish. It makes sense to do it

Notice the point at which I start the cast (left photo). My rod is around the eleven and twelve o'clock position. When I have released the line, my rod is around the two and three o'clock position (right photo).

this way based on your ability to manipulate and finesse fish around obstacles as you fight them. I will be describing right-handed fighters, so left-handed fishermen should reverse the descriptions.

The lower half of your rod is called the "butt". Place your right hand on the butt and close your hand over it and the bottom of your reel (the seat) at the same time. Your forefinger and index finger should be above the seat of the reel, and the last two fingers should be below it, with your thumb wrapped around the index finger. With your left hand, flip the "carriage" or "bail" over and extend your forefinger so that it is pointed out, and place the line at the tip of your finger. The best way to describe what happens next is to imagine that the rod is an extension of your finger: Take the rod and drape it over your right shoulder while at the same time keeping your line on the tip of your finger. Your rod should be between 8 to 10 1/2 feet long, and you should get into the habit of casting with one hand and not two. While the rod is over your shoulder look out in front of you and envision where you want the end of your line to land in the water. Throw your right hand forward, as though you were about to throw something. Imagine that the rod follows a pattern that is similar to a clock. Directly behind you is nine o'clock straight and in front of you is three

o'clock. Begin your cast at eleven o'clock and throw your hand forward until you get to about one or two o'clock, then retract your finger ever so slightly while continuing your forward motion with the rod. You will have to envision the strength you need to attain your desired distance, the outcome should be relatively the same. Your leader should end up somewhere directly in front of you, not off to the side.

If you're having trouble at first, don't worry about it. It takes a little time to perfect the art, but I promise it won't take long before you master this. Do not cast with two arms, it will have a grave impact on the direction of your line. Focus on the cast. The line should be on the very tip of your casting finger (forefinger), almost to the point of falling off. Don't worry if it does, just make a small adjustment and cast again. Gravity is a good friend of the fisherman.

As soon as the tip of your line hits the water, reach over to the reel with your left hand and flip the "bail" back into its original closed position. Let your leader and lead sink a few seconds. Begin to reel in your slack as the line approaches you, coming downstream. Be sure not to reel too much in, you don't want your leader line at the surface of the water; rather, you want it somewhere near the bottom near the rocks and structure. When the line starts to rise as it passes you, and gains speed in the water, either let it "free bail" or reel the line in and cast out again. Free-bailing is when you let your line go far downstream by flipping over the bail while keeping your fingers in constant contact with the line. In time, you will be able to cast out at any angle you want.

What the Hit Feels Like

It is the thing that haunts all fishermen who go drift fishing. It was what made me ask so many questions before I ever decided to drift fish. It's the one thing that every fisherman agreed upon; the "hit" was indistinguishable from bumping into rocks or getting tangled in a snag. My discovery was that it wasn't the "hit" that was the issue; rather, the enigma lay in distinguishing the types of "hits".

Many skilled fishermen told me that you had to watch your line because sometimes the hit was so subtle your only indication of a hit was your line "pausing" and then moving on down the river. Some told me that the hit would feel like a "tick" which would mimic the same feeling you would get from a small trout hitting your line. Still others told me that the hit could never be discerned because the fish were so intelligent they would

take an offering into their mouths and simply move backwards without disturbing your line, letting go of it once it made the distinction that the lure was artificial.

I knew that the men whom I had spoken with had a good working knowledge of what to do and what not to do, so my intimidation grew. But rather than succumb to a melancholy state, I decided that if I was going to go fishing I should first overcome the major obstacles that plague most fishermen so I would not become a statistic.

First, I considered the point of watching the line through the drift. Many fishermen had told me that the more invisible your line was, the better your chance would be that the fish would not be spooked and would more than likely pick up your offering. But if the line is invisible, how am I going to watch it as it travels through the drift? It made sense to me that if the line was invisible to the fish, then it would surely be invisible to me.

I went to a sporting goods store to look at the lines that were available anyway. I looked for a very long time because there were so many from which to choose. Each company swore that their line was the most invisible. I spoke with a few people in the store and they all had

their own ideas as to which line to use. I thought that I might buy a variety of lines just to be safe, until I saw one that was quite different; I stopped cold in my tracks. The line was the exact opposite of everything I had seen or had even heard; itwas called X-T Solar And it was extremely-visible fluorescent green line. It was at that point that I had an epiphany. I knew that each person whom I had talked to was referring to the leader and not the mainline. "You don't catch fish with the mainline", which was the very thing that I had been told would be necessary to watch as my leader went through the drift. I reasoned that the fish would not care enough to be spooked by this line and would inevitably be more concerned about the offering I would make, the visible line would be regarded as debris and the fish would move out of the way, just enough for it to pass by. It made sense that the more visible my mainline was, the easier it would be for me to watch for hesitations and complete stops. It was a major breakthrough. I bought a couple of spools of the line and left without discussing it with anyone because I was sure they would take issue, discouraging me further.

I considered the olfactory capabilities of steelhead and salmon. I found that approximately 1/3 of their brain was dedicated to their sense of smell, and as far as I was concerned that didn't sound like the intelligent creature so many fishermen had described. I believed I was onto something, so I decided to go to the Puyallup River with a friend of mine and put my reasoning to the test. We got there a short time after sunrise and began to fish. I knew that it would take me a short time to become familiar with the bottom of the river by "gliding". The first time I drifted a glide, I saw my line hesitate at some point in the direction of two o'clock. We were drifting from left to right. I cast out again and saw that my line did the same thing but not quite the same place that it had the first time. On the third cast, I was prepared. I anticipated that my line would hesitate at some point and I was ready. As my line went through the water, I watched it hesitate for the final time and as it did I pulled back as sharply as I could, setting the hook into my very first steelhead. It was all over the water and in the air. The fight was exactly as I had been told it would be. I had the fish onto shore a few minutes later, where I "tailed" it to land it. Ron, my friend, came over to me to ask me what the hit had felt like. I told him that everyone had been right and wrong all along. I never did feel the hit; the only thing that I knew for sure was that I had made the right decision about getting the bright line. The line was highly visible and allowed me to see it slow down as it went down the river. It was then that I knew to set the hook. It was something Ron could not embrace. Watching the lure was just as vital as feeling it. Ron just couldn't believe it was that simple. He never did catch a fish that day. I went on to catch one more about an hour later.

But as to the mystique of drift fishing, I was sure that many of the questions fishermen had could be answered by applying science instead of believing that luck and years played a key role. An inappropriate mystique clouds the recreational fishing industry, and that too is a major problem all beginning fishermen will have to overcome.

The premise to understanding the hit is relatively simple. The hit can be the line slowing down during the drift when it had not on the previous cast, or it can be that the line stops completely. It might be that the line becomes just a little bit heavier than it had from the last drift, that is to say, as it goes through the water the line neither stops nor slows down, but seems just to move in a way that makes the water feel thicker. You can feel the difference on the line as it rests on your fingertip throughout the drift. Occasionally the hit will feel like a couple of quick taps on your line as though someone were touching the tip of your rod. Ultimately the hit is anything that is anomalous during the drift; to find these anomolies drift through a body of water and familiarize yourself with it in just a few minutes. When something changes in the way the line feels. or if it slows or stops, set the hook, because only a fish can cause these changes in the way your line travels through the water.

Setting the Hook

Setting the hook is the first step in fighting a fish. Bear in mind that setting the hook needs to be done only one time. You don't do it twice or three times, you just do it once. I have seen fishermen set the hook on a fish as many as five times; there is absolutely no or reason for this. When you think you have a fish on the end of your line, pull back sharply; if you feel any resistance, hold your rod so that the line is taut and the tip of your rod is bent high out over your head and wait for the fish to run. Then hold on.

The gums on a steelhead are extremely soft by comparison to any salmon. Even a very small hook will penetrate the gum line. It is because the gum line is so soft that you should only set the hook

once. If you pull two or more times you run the risk of pulling the hook out of its mouth even if the hook is set deep in the jaw. If you are bottom bouncing or just plain gliding, when in doubt about whether or not you have a fish hitting your line, set the hook! Occasionally I will even set the hook when I think it's a small fish (a shaker), only to be surprised by a nice fifteen-pounder. Set your hook once and have confidence in your abilities to fight the fish, and you will land it.

Setting the hook involves knowing the function of the "butt" of your rod. By placing your forearm and elbow directly in line with the butt, you increase your hook-setting power immensely. You will set the hook more firmly and diminish the chances of losing a fish by not relying solely on your wrist, giving you more time to worry about fighting the fish as opposed to losing it. Notice the placement of my forearm, elbow, and the butt of the rod as I set the hook on a chinook salmon.

While fighting the fish, your rod tip should remain up, illustrated by my position in the photo on the lower right. Your rod should remain at about a 45-degree angle for as long as possible. I know that it's not always possible to keep it at that angle, especially when it comes time to land a fish, but you can put the rod somewhere on the ground, net the fish, or have a fishing buddy help you land the fish. If you are going to land the fish by yourself,

watch the tip of your rod so that it does-n't bend sharply at the tip. Rods were never meant to be in that position and the pressure of the sharp bend in such a small area could cause it to snap off. The most important thing to remember when you are fighting a fish is to keep the rod up and never let the rod point directly towards the fish. The direct pressure of the line to the reel could split the reel guide, or the direct pressure could cause your drag to fail completely rendering it useless. You could end up losing the fish, breaking your reel, and going home early.

Fighting the Fish

Once you have the fish on, remain calm. Overly anxious fishermen lose fish. Know the terrain underneath the water before you fish the river, and if you don't, there are some things you can do to make sure that you will land the fish.

Do not lower the tip of your rod if the fish is running deep. There are boulders and snags all over many riverbeds. The more line you have in the water, the greater the likelihood that your line will tangle around one of them and you will lose the fish. If the fish is running in shal-low water, and you know it for a fact, then and only then do you put your rod tip towards the surface of the water, keeping your rod bent at the same time. By keep-ing your rod down at this point you accomplish two things. First, by lowering the tip when the water is shallow, you do not inspire the fish to jump; if it doesn't jump, then the line will be fast-hooked to the jaw and you will be more likely, than not, to land the fish. Second, if it does jump, immediately put your rod tip in and below the water surface so that no slack will be given to the fish. By doing this, you cause constant resistance on the line without over-pulling and ripping the hook out of the fish. As soon as it goes back into the water, bring your rod tip back up to a 45-degree angle and contin-ue to fight. The only other reason to put your rod tip low or actually underneath, the surface of the water is to stop the fish from stripping off your line completely.

Not many people will tell you how much they enjoyed having all of their line taken by the biggest steelhead they ever hooked. The way to combat a fish, and to turn it around and keep it out of the whitewater, is to put your rod tip in the water and give the fish as much slack as you can by flipping your bail open and letting the fish run. By flipping your bail you actually cause your line to get ahead of the fish, and also cause resistance in the opposite direction. Steelhead have an intrinsic sense that tells them to pull in the opposite direction of any resistance by a hook-set. Since the resistance is coming from a belly forming in the line in front of it, the fish will haul ass back up the river to where you are. Because the slack that was created gives it free reign to go very fast back towards you, this is a critical time in the fight.

Remember the various snags I told you about earlier? Your line is now down in the water with them, and if you have any hope of catching the fish—and not the snags—reel like crazy. If you can control your excitement, you will be better off. Once the fish has come back to where you are, keep your rod tip in accordance to the depth of the fish and play it out. It's to your benefit not to try to haul it in (horse the fish). It will tire soon enough, and will come in on its own. Let the fish do the work. As long as you have complete control of the rod, the fish will do whatever you want it to do. When it begins to get tired and comes into shore, be sure that it's not trying to snooker you. Many times I have seen a steelhead come to shore only to bolt at the first thing it

touches, which causes your line to go slack enough for the fish to snap it and swim away. The best approach is to get into the water with the fish and grab it by the tail, if you don't have a net. This process is called "tailing".

Tailing

Tailing a fish is not difficult once you know the mechanics of the process. The bigger the species you are going after, the easier it is to tail a fish. Chinook, chum, and steelhead are relatively easy to tail, but the smaller species like coho, sockeye, and pinks are much more difficult because of the smaller size of the tail wrist (the caudal area of the tail). To counter this problem, use either a soft towel or wool gloves for gripping the smaller species.

The act of tailing a fish is not overly complicated. Get into the water up to your knees as the fish tires to give you the advantage of not having to bend down. Keep your rod tip up high and away from the fish as it gets close to you. The greater the distance the tip is away from the body, the better. You don't want to cause a sharp bend in the tip, this might snap it in two. Next, I align the fish in front of me with the head facing away from my body to make sure that the tail is within easy grasp. With a firm and confident motion, I grab the fish by the tail and hold it in place for just a moment or two. Ordinarily

the fish will thrash about a few times, but then becomes immobile, and I am then able to release it back into the water.

Catch and Release

The delicate nature of the gills did not occur to me until I read somewhere that the smallest stroke of them can cause irreparable damage. The only way for fish to get oxygen is to wash water through their mouths and over their gills. Stringing up a fish and then putting it back into the water is a terrible idea. The trauma to the gills will kill the fish. It is a crime against nature to catch all the fish you can and then keep most of them. The main reason I fish is for the fight, and then I resuscitate them and put them back into the water.

One of the most important things to remember when you are about to land a fish is that it should not leave the water. If you feel that you need to net the fish, make sure it stays in the water. The net should be made of cloth and not the plastic kind that prevails on the market. Water temperature permitting, I almost always take the hook out while the head is still under water to make sure that it continues

to breathe. The photo above shows me "tailing" a fish while leaving it's head beneath the surface while I retrieve the hook.

It would be unresonable to assume that the entire body of the fish will be able to constantly remain submerged, however, it is important to make sure that the head and gills remain under water while you take the hook out. Be at the ready to take photgraphs so the amount of time the fish might be out of the water is minimized, thusly diminishing the prospect of the fish experiencing shock anymore than it needs to.

When you are ready to put the fish back, be sure to watch it as you let it go. If for any reason it flounders and does not swim away, then grasp it gently by the tail wrist and move it back and forth slowly until it looks as though it will move off on its own. If you want to take pictures, do so as quickly as possible. Use the length of your rod for dimensional photographs. The formula for determining the weight of a fish is length x girth squared divided by 800. This will give you a very accurate calculation of what the fish weighed without having to hurt it.

Understanding Fish

Dawn to Dusk

The sense (visual and olfactory) acuity of a fish is incredible, and very different from the way we perceive things. Look at these two pictures. The one on the left was taken at the Cowlitz River just before daybreak. The fisherman didn't use anything that glowed, and he didn't use anything overly remarkable to attract the fish. He knew when the bite would be on. More often than not, that means getting out into the woods long before daylight. The photo on the right shows me holding a fish that I had caught with an experimental rig. Though it was the dead of night, I was sure that I didn't need a "glow rig" setup. Knowing that the area had been pressured, I used a size-ten cerise-pink corkie and yarn with shrimp oil. It was an experiment on the abilities of the steelhead olfactory. I landed this fish in one drift through a seam.

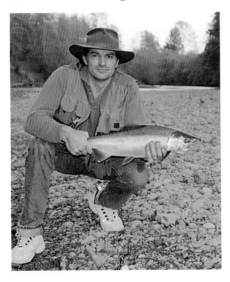

Many times I have fished in the evening and morning with just a sliver of light. Because of the diminished lighting, fish cannot see you, but they can see and smell whatever offering you put in front of them. They will slam it, more often than not, with vigor. Because they do not perceive danger, they focus on the task of feeding rather than pressure from fishermen during daylight hours.

One of two things will make them take your offering consistently in the early morning and evening, more so than any other time. If they are spawning, they will hit your offering, in an effort to keep their area free of debris, or if they are feeding they will also hit your offering with gusto. In either case, it's an excellent idea to be on the water when they feel the freedom to behave like fish, and are not focusing on the pressure of human presence. Another thing to consider is when you can see a steelhead, it has seen you long before you ever saw it. If you can get down to the river without being seen by any fish, your chances of catching them will improve dramatically.

The thing about steelhead is that they do not have the intelligence that most fishermen attribute to them. I am not disparaging the magnificence of these great creatures but rather speaking plainly. Steelhead are highly instinctive. The goals of any fish are pretty simple: survive and propagate; if you can understand what that entails, you will be a very successful fisherman.

Pressure

This is the quickest way to make sure the fish don't bite. "Pressuring" fish is something that people "do" and is not a naturally occurring phenomenon. An inordinate number of fishermen within the same location is the most intense kind of pressure fish can experience. this pressure is commonly referred to as combat fishing. Imagine that you are a fish trying to get upriver, but before you can do that you have to pass a gauntlet of fishermen with many lines in the water. Seeing all of those fishermen, coupled with all of the foreign objects in the water, will turn you off to the idea of biting into anything.

There a couple of things the angler can do to make pressured water, like in these photos, produce fish. First, look at the fishermen near you. Find those who are catching fish and watch for their offering and then try to replicate what they're using. If none of the fishermen are catching fish, then find out what they are all using and don't use any of it. Next, rather than stand in the same position as the fishermen along the bank, change it up and step further into the water or step back from those around you, Cast further or shorter; or change the direction of the cast. One of these methods should produce hits.

Somewhere along the bank of combat fishing, you will find a spot that is not occupied for a long stretch. It could be several dozen feet or several hundred. Under the pressure of combat fishing, fish gravitate to areas that are less pressured, regardless of the terrain or depth of the river. I maintain that it's a good idea to go to areas with combat fishing. They're great placea to learn many facets of fishing.

Spawning

Steelhead have the innate need to spawn, just like salmon. The difference between the two is that steelhead return to the sea and salmon die very shortly after spawning. As steelhead mature in the spawning

Hole punched into gill plate for tracking spawned fish.

cycle, they develop deep colors, most notably, pink and then red on their cheeks and an accompanying red line down the length of their bodies that starts at the gill plate. They tend to move up the river at night, and hold their positions during the day.

For tracking purposes, state hatcheries have designed a gillplate hole-punching system that allows state workers to identify those fish that have spawned from those that have not. Those that have the punch are finished with the spawning cycle and those that don't, are not. Fish that have these punched holes are called "punched" fish. The thing about steelhead that are either just about to spawn, or have just finished their mating cycle, are not very good fighters. If you have caught a very dark fish or you have just landed a very skinny, tired-looking fish, put it back into the water, for a couple of reasons. First, steelhead are renowned for

the fight they put up, that is, until just before and just after they spawn. Second, the meat of a steelhead at this time is not very good at all, in fact I dare to compare the meat to that of a dying salmon. You might hear someone tell you that a dark or skinny fish is good for "smoking", but don't believe it. For the enhancement of the recreational fishing industry and for posterity, it's best if you put a spawned-out fish back into the water.

The Value of a Fish Scale

Scales are the only protection a fish has against disease and injury. When a single scale is removed from a fish it becomes susceptible to disease and injury. Fungus and parasites attack points of injury where a scale has dropped and don't stop attacking once started. In an attempt to alleviate the discomfort, a fish will scrape its body on rocks and other abrasive surfaces. In doing so, they lose even more

Lateral Line

scales, offering more area for the disease to spread, and eventually they are overcome and die.

All fish have a "lateral line" that runs the length of their body and functions as a means of stability for the fish as it swims through the water. This porous organ is a means by which they can detect water currents, vibrations, and pressure changes. Once this lateral line is disturbed—either from internal injuries, such as swim bladder disease, constipation, or various forms of Ich disease, or external injuries, such as disturbance of scales by careless fishermen, wounds from seals or bears, it can never recover.

Poor handling of a fish by a fisherman can kill it. When you release a fish

Looking up from underneath the water's surface, the refractive qualities of the water's constant undulating distort my features.

from your hook, if at all possible, the fish should never leave the water. If practicing catch and release, always use barbless hooks for easier removal. Above all, you should never use a net. Nets are the number-one cause of lost scales. There is nothing wrong with netting a fish, dragging a fish to shore, or using barbed hooks if you intend to keep the fish.

Once you decide you're going to keep a fish, follow through. Do not string up a fish and then release it back in the water.

If you catch a bigger fish and you want to catch and release, put back the bigger fish and be a good sport. Paying attention to the needs of the fish will ensure that we all have the opportunity to catch fish in the future.

Refraction and Perspective

Did you know that seeing through the water's surface is just as difficult for the fish as it is for you? It is equally distorted from above the surface and below it. The closer a fish is to the surface of the water, the more difficult it is for the fish to see out of it. Conversely, the deeper, it is the more easily it can see. To give you some idea of what the fish might see if you were directly above it, I have taken some underwater photos.

Refraction is displacement of light rays through a prism; in this case it refers to water, and the perception of objects as seen through the surface of the water. This refraction causes images to appear in places they are not. That is to say, the rock or fish you see may not be as big or as close as you might think because the refractive ability of the water's surface distorting the location and relative size of these objects.

Practice

Understanding What You Are Looking At

Understanding the surface of the water is very important in realizing whether or not the section of river you are on is capable of holding fish. The best way to practice is to go to water that is both clear and void of fish. If the water is smooth and has current, try placing large boulders in it and watch what happens to the surface. Make notes on how the water moves over the rock and affects the surface. Notice the difference between the two.

Take a trip to your local hatchery. The best time to go is when fish are migrating into it. If you don't know when they start coming in, ask the people who work there, they will be happy to tell you when to come back. When the fish are in, they are kept in giant concrete pools called "ponds". Though you may marvel at the amount of fish you see, it's what the fish are doing to the water as they breach the surface that you need to pay special attention to. Because there will be so many

fish, focus on one fish at a time. Watch as the water crests over the back of a fish, recall what it looks like. Recalling what the water surface looks like as fish are directly underneath the surface is a critical element to consider when reading water. Make sure to set aside time to go to a hatchery and watch water that holds fish. In the field, most rivers will not run as clear as a hatchery's. Colored water is still water, and the fundamentel rules of water dynamics apply. Knowing what the surface looks like as fish hold in any given part of the river will help you to spot them even in water that has zero visibility.

It will take a few trips to the hatchery to memorize the nuances. Consider an area of the pool that does not have fish near the surface, and then compare what you have seen to fish that are even deeper. When the fish are so deep that you cannot see them, then look for water that seems to slightly "boil". The only time you will see water that boils in very slow-moving water is when there's a deep pool which is holding fish.

Spotting Fish

If you focus on spotting a fish in the water the same way you would if the fish were in your hand, you will be sorely disappointed. Water refraction (bent light) and clarity conspire against human optics. I have taken these photos to demonstrate how to spot fish. Look for the silhouette of a vague shadow and watch for it to move, this is a sign that what you are looking at is not a rock in the water.

Understanding how to spot fish lies somewhere between art and science. In perfect conditions you will be able to see fish in the water. The sun has to be high in the sky, the shadows directly at your feet, and the fish have to be holding where you are looking. It's not impossible for these conditions to take place, but you might only get out a few times in your life if you are depending on these conditions to present themselves in order to spot fish.

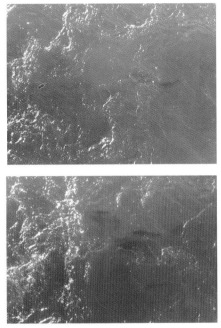

Above are two photos to aid in spotting fish. It's not the easy-to-see fish I want to focus on, but the more difficult ones. We would all like to see fish easily, however, dark spots in the water are the best fishermen can hope for when it comes to spotting them. As you spot fish in the river be aware that you may not always see fish clearly like you would in a fish tank. Changing barometric pressures conspire against the human eye with colored water from rainfall and glare from the sun. Shadows and water surface movements are the things to look for when spotting fish. Believe it or not, there are a couple dozen fish in these two pictures alone. Practice looking at the photos, and then look for the more difficult ones and you will be ready to spot fish along the bank, or against the side of rocks, boulders, backeddies, riffles, and deep pools. There are some more difficult pictures to help you hone your skill at spotting fish.

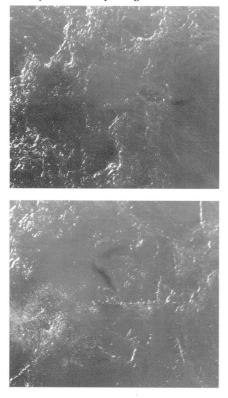

The four photos above are broken down into two columns. The left photo is duplicated with a copy to the right of it. Cover up the second column, and spot the fish in the first column. Each photo becomes progressively harder. When you can spot the fish in the last photo, you will be able to spot fish in very muddy water in the field.

In the beginning, go to popular places to practice this skill. Ask as many questions as you need to. This doesn't mean you'll always get the answer you are looking for, but sometimes you can learn a valuable piece of information you didn't

have before. Most of the time, you will find that many people are amiable and anxious to help. Take this woman in the picture, at the bottom of the page for example. She's in waders, has a great rod and reel, but knew very little about fishing.

After watching her for some time, I asked her if I could help. She was trying to cast the same way that someone might if he or she were using a spinning reel when in fact she was using a baitcaster. She had

fifty-pound test and no weight on her line. By spending just a few short minutes with her, she got the knowledge she needed to come back another day completely prepared, and be more productive.

Recon

Before I put in any real fishing time on a new system, I make a recon trip to investigate the variables that I would not be prepared for had I not gone in the first place. I consider the level of the water, the terrain, and accessibility. I prefer to make most of my trips in summer when most of the rivers are running low and clear, as this gives me a good idea of what to expect in the fall and winter months. During summer I can see where potential holds will be when the water is higher. I consider how far I will have to walk, and consider the precautions I should take when the walk "could" become more precarious in the snow and rain. If it looks like it could be too much trouble, either because it is too far or too dangerous, then I just enjoy my day there and go somewhere else the next day. You cannot be too careful on a recon trip, be even more so in the colder months to come. Be honest with yourself when you go on recon trips; if it looks like it could be too much trouble, then go somewhere else.

A great way to find out the history of the river is to seek out the local store in the vicinity of the system you want to fish. The people who work there will, more often than not, know of some great fishing holes.

In the photo on the right, I am standing above a potential hole in the Hamma-Hamma River. Based on the height of the boulders I am standing on and the speed of the water below me, I perceive it to be a bad place to fish when the

water rises. The safety factor here is practically non-existent. That being the case, I decided to go further down river and consider less dangerous options.

Steelhead can be caught most of the year., but the river systems that offer them have their own agenda. The months vary, as do the size of the fish. Though difficult, steelhead can be caught during the winter months in the early morning and then again at dusk. Because a successful season is based on when the fish decide to hit your lure, you are at the whims of their disposition. Knowing the "system" is one of the necessary keys to catching fish. Understanding the nuances of a river will forecast sreasons and viability to fish it. knowing where and when to fish any river will streamline productive trips. It is also the smaller things that make up the trip that are just as vital as knowing the larger more general aspects of a river.

You will have the advantage over other fishermen if you know the proper angles at which to make your presentations. Sometimes angle positioning may be the only thing that makes the difference. Taking a step or two in any direction can help if you're not getting any hits. Knowing what the terrain looks like in low-water conditions will tell you which way to step and cast in order to get your gear down to where the fish are holding.

First-Timers

Kyle is in the photo below. I took Kyle to the Humtulips for the coho and chum run. I prepped him and gave him some final things to consider before we got there. Ironically, it was the last thing I told him that helped him to set the hook on this beautiful chum on his very first cast. I said he should think about the weight resistance of his line as it went through the water, and that if the weight of it seemed lethargic and unfamiliar to him, he should set the hook. I told him that sometimes all a fish does is hold the corkie in its mouth before releasing it. He watched his highly visible line and felt the weight of it as he drifted his line for the first time that morning. When he felt an unfamiliar resistance, he set the hook. It was his very first time on that system.

Mike is in the picture on the top of the next page. He paid mindful attention to what I had to say and followed through by going out and getting the things that he needed. Mike told me about trips that he had taken to Alaska, where the fishing and instruction were non-existent. Knowing that he needed to become familiar with all the necessary elements, I took him to combat fish at Hoodsport, Washington. It was a great place for him to learn how to fight fish based on the abundance of available fish.

I believe that we should all exercise free will and thinking, but my applications necessitate that each and every person follow through to the exact letter of my instructions for them to work, and that is exactly what he did. The very first

biting; I won't sit on the bank and wishing I could catch a fish when others around me are.

Drift fishing is a rough sport, and you get out of it what you put into it. When the fish are biting you need to keep fishing until you know that the bite is off. Conversing while you are fishing is fine, social interaction will not deter fish from your hook, as long as your line is in the water and you're paying close attention to what you are doing.

time we went drifting for steelhead he got one, and in the photo he is holding up one of the best-looking steelhead you could hope to land, whatever your skill level.

The man on the right is Marcus. I am pleased to have had the opportunity to take him out. Prior to fishing with me his experiences were limited to saltwater fishing. It took me some time to convince him that he would be able to catch a fish in a freshwater system.

It will happen now and again that a fisherman will have a tough time getting his gear into some fish, and Marcus just happened to be one of those unfortunate enough to go through it. To be honest it took him three trips to get his fish, but he did, and there he is displaying his catch. I thought about his lack of hookups and came to the conclusion that his efforts were rewarded accordingly.

When I go fishing I go to catch fish and nothing else. That is not to say that I am so focused on catching fish that I don't think about anything else, but from a distance you might think that.

I won't stop to eat when the fish are

Not Getting a Hit?

S horten your leader: consider water clarity and barometric pressure.

■ **Lengthen your leader:** if the clarity is gin clear, your leader should be longer than usual.

■ **Reduce the weight:** occasionally fish will gravitate near the surface. By reducing the weight you don't need to increase your leader length.

■ **Increase your weight:** if the water is moving your offering too fast, you might want to increase the amount of weight so that the fish are able to take a longer look at your offering.

■ **Change scent:** when fish are pressured into avoiding scent, it is to your benefit to change your scent on the

corkie. Be sure to change the corkie as well so the scent that was on it will not taint the new scent as well.

■ **Change your position in the water:** even moving as little of as foot can make the difference. Positioning for presentation is very important.

■ **Change your corkie to another color or size:** pressure can make fish very finicky. If you're not getting a fish right away then it might be the color or size of your corkie. Of course this is contingent upon the fact that you are fishing the water correctly.

■ **If you are combat fishing:** and no one is catching any fish, find out what the predominant offering is and make sure you don't use it: take a look around and make sure that you are not doing the same as others fishing near you. Sometimes changing one small thing can make the difference between when and if you get a strike.

■ **Is the water holding any fish:** be absolutely sure that the water is holding fish. There is always some way to discern whether or not the water you are fishing is capable of holding fish.

Before You Leave for the River

- ❏ Base your leader's length on weather conditions, water clarity, and water height
- ❏ Have enough weights, both slinky and pencil lead
- ❏ Swivels
- ❏ Toothpicks
- ❏ Beads
- ❏ Fish scent
- ❏ Extra corkies
- ❏ Yarn
- ❏ Hooks
- ❏ Scissors
- ❏ Fingernail clippers
- ❏ Needlenose pliers
- ❏ Flashlight
- ❏ License
- ❏ Regulation handbook
- ❏ Hat
- ❏ Gloves
- ❏ Camera
- ❏ Fillet knife
- ❏ Stringer
- ❏ Warm clothing
- ❏ Neoprene waders, or hip boots
- ❏ Rag wool socks to go on the outside of neoprene waders
- ❏ Gravel guard to go over the socks over the waders
- ❏ First-aid kit
- ❏ Check the weather
- ❏ Road conditions
- ❏ Calculate the drive time
- ❏ Establish approximate time of arrival and departure
- ❏ Check the hydrograph station (on the Internet) for water height of the system you will fish

Weather

Weather Forecasts

With the advent of the Internet, finding out what the weather will be has never been easier. Weather plays a very important role in the behavior of steelhead. The colder the water gets, the more lethargic the fish become, and the harder it is to tempt them into hitting your hook. The warmer it is, the easier it is to tempt them and the harder they will hit. It could take a few trips to understand precisely how the weather affects the water you want to fish, but there are some general rules you can follow.

hard to entice because inevitably they become lethargic because of the drop in temperature. In this case you must be ready to be diverse in your presentations. Large to medium profiles will be needed as a standard procedure; however, if the barometric pressure is high you will also need smaller offerings for your profiles as well. One of the things you need to consider is you might need a small profile and a short leader to tempt the fish to strike. Even though the water might be crystal clear, you will need short leaders because the pressure will drive the fish down around six inches to a foot from

Cloudy/Partial Sun	Sat May 1 1 AM	Sat May 1 2 AM	Sat May 1 3 AM	Sat May 1 4 AM	Sat May 1 5 AM	Sat May 1 6 AM	Sat May 1 7 AM
Forecast	Cloudy	Cloudy	Cloudy	Partial Clearing	Cloudy	Fog	Fog/Clearing
Temperature	49	48	48	49	51	51	53
Wind	SW 10mph	S 7mph	SW 8mph	SE 2	SE 4mph	S 1mph	Calm

In the fall and winter months, the warmer it is, the more likely the water will rise and the muddier it will be; bearing that in mind, your leader will be shorter and the profile will be larger. The weight system you use will be determined by the water current and substructure. Whether the barometric pressure falls or not, when the freezing level falls then so too will the water level of the river, and water clarity will increase. There is a paradox you will encounter.

Though the water will clear and the level of the river will fall, the fish are still

the bed of the river. Consider how warm you might be in the weather you are fishing in; the warmer it is for you, the more active you are going to be, and the same applies to fish. The next step is to consider water level and clarity.

Falling and Rising Waters (USGS Hydrograph)

Water flow is a very important factor to consider when you decide to fish. Water flow can dictate when a fish will bite and when it will not. When the water in a river rises, the increase in volume will

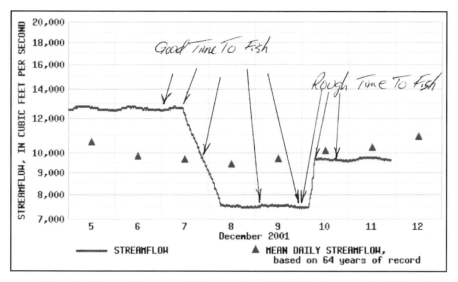

turn fish off. Fish tend to stop biting because they are looking for a place to hold by the edges of the river to wait for the water to slow down. A fish knows that when the water rises it brings debris down the river that has the potential to harm it, so, rather than brave the gauntlet they gravitate to the edges and wait for the water to stabilize. Even then it is hard to get a fish to bite, even though the water has begun to stabilize, there is still a great deal of harmful debris floating down the river.

If you fish soon after the water has risen, look for small back-eddies and fish very close to the water's edge. Knowing the water level of the river before you go is easy, thanks to the wealth of information available on the Internet. Type in the key word "hydrograph" and you will find a plethora of sites. An up-to-date hydrograph lets you know in advance what the water conditions will be like. Above is a diagram of changing water levels.

Mean Daily Streamflow

When the water is stable and falling, it's a good time to hit the water; however, when the water goes from stable to rising and then stable again for a short period of time, it is difficult to get the fish to bite. This graph was taken from the Cowlitz Mayfield Dam record archives provided by the USGS. Though the Cowlitz's water level is governed by a dam, you can apply the same thinking to rivers that are glacially fed. There are many stations that keep up-to-the-hour reports like this one.

Barometric Pressure

The barometric pressure on this day was extremely high. It's important to consider because a rising barometer affects the way a fish behaves. You can be sure that the higher the barometer, the more skittish the fish are going to be because visibility increases dramatically. Any fish you're able to see can see you as well. A high-pressure system typically means that the sun is out and there's no chance of precipitation. This kind of weather drives fish down to deeper water. The deeper the water, the brighter your lures and baits need to be. A flashy offering will entice a fish to strike more vigorously in the warming temperatures than they would in a low-pressure system. The flash of any lure is to do nothing more than get the attention of any nearby fish.

79

When the water is that clear and warm, I try to stand back away from the fish and cast out to them from a decent distance. With a pair of polarized glasses you will be able to see the fish from a greater distance. This distance allows the fish to disregard you and will take the pressure off them.

Here I am fishing a low-pressure system. The whole time I was fishing this water, I never saw a fish jump. It was a cold winter day. I understood that on a low-pressure system that fish tend to be less spooky and easier to catch, but because the weather was so cold that also meant that they would be lethargic and less apt to strike with vigor.

Behind me you can see two currents in the water. One surface is slicker and greener. Take a good look at it and you will see that it is a pool just before it hits the fast water, and that is where the fish lay in conditions such as these. Ordinarily on a low pressure front, the fish come closer to the surface because visibility is more limited and they are less easily spooked, but because it was also cold, I

knew they could be down deeper where the water was warmer. By gliding I was able to get my gear down to this nice hen that slammed me so hard for a brief moment I thought she would rip the rod right out of my hand.

Winter conditions like these are much more intimidating to fishermen, so more often than not there are few of them around. It doesn't take too much effort to stay warm, and the reward for going out into this weather can be a heart-pounding experience that will easily keep you warm for the rest of the day.

It was my understanding of pressure systems that allowed me to anticipate what gear would be needed to catch fish in both of these situations.

Wind

Your line in the wind acts very much like a sail. The more intense the wind, the more your line will billow. The line billowing (line belly) is what will destroy your ability to percieve a strike when a fish picks up your hook. Let me give you another example.

80

Wind/Rain Temp Velocity/Wind
50% 63 South to North-east at 18mph

Think of your line functioning like a tight wire with two cans at either end, like when you were a kid playing "telephone" with your friends. The tighter the line was, the better you could hear the voice of your friend, and the more slack you gave it, the less you could hear. This same rule applies to your fishing line. Having belly in your line will not allow for a quick hook-set. The only way you are going to feel a fish when you have any kind of belly or bow in your line is if it slams you hard. Most of the time, steelhead "mouth" whatever they intend to hit and

you need to understand that the tactile sensation is vital. If you don't feel the fish, and you cannot see your line stop in the water, you will not get the fish.

Knowing the wind speed is just as important as all ofthe other elements. Do not fish an area with a wind velocity greater than twelve miles per hour. The wind cannot sustain itself for extended periods of time if twelve is the maximum speed, but, if the area you intend to fish has a minimum speed of twelve you are better off going somewhere else, or just waiting for a better day to fish.

Filleting Your Catch

Steps for Filleting Your Fish

The process of the fillet is not a complicated one, but it is one that I have never seen discussed with any accurate fervor.

The first thing that should be done when keeping a fish for filleting is to gill the fish in the field. The quality of the meat radically improves with the removal of the blood, and "gilling" is the most productive way to make that happen.

Lift the gill plate and pull out one or two gills, wait for the blood to evacuate. The next step in the fillet process is done at home soon after you leave the field. You want to transport the fish as quickly as possible, or pack it in ice if you're not in a hurry to get home.

There are a few things that will make sure you are safe to work on the fish without cutting yourself:

1) you need a large enough area that you won't have to struggle to manipulate the fish;

2) you need a large garbage bag for disposal of the waste;

3) have a few good dry rags around so your grip on the fish will make it safe for you to do the fillet;

4) for cleanup purposes you need a good anti-bacterial soap to wash everything that you and the fish touch;

5) finally you need an appropriately-sized fillet knife that complements the size of your catch.

1. The very first thing that needs to be done is to remove the entrails. Score the belly of the fish by beginning at the anus and working your way to the underside of the jaw. Keep in mind as you do this that the knife will not have to go very deep, as the skin of the fish is not that thick.

2. The knife cut will stop in between the gill plates underneath the jaw. If you are not sure how far you should go, remove the knife and look for the heart of the fish. If you don't see it, then you haven't gone far enough, if you do, stop and begin the removal process.

3. Begin at the back end of the fish and work your way forward by only partially removing the entrails. Removing the insides of the fish in this way is efficient and cuts down on the cleanup effort.

4. Be cautious about this step. You want to focus your attention at the very beginning of the esophagus (throat). With your left hand, feel as far up the esophagus as you can. When you can't go any farther bring your hand back a couple of inches and hold the esophagus with a firm grip. With the knife in your right hand, score and then cut the esophagus as close to the heart, as you are able. By focusing on the placement of the heart and with your left hand as far back as it is, it should be safe for you to make the cut without the possibility of getting cut in the process.

5. Now that you're ready for filleting, prepare the scores you need to help guide your knife. Take a rag in your left hand and grab the caudal area of the fish and hold it. With the knife in your right hand, score the wrist area of the fish in a crescent moon shape. This will give your knife a finishing point after the next few steps.

6. Flip the fish so that the head is closest to your left hand. Again with a rag in your left hand, lift the pectoral fin so that it is up and away from the body of the fish. With the knife in your right hand, score the fish in a crescent fashion starting at the belly side where your knife stopped just underneath the jaw of the fish when you made the cut for removing the entrails.

7. As a guide, follow the gill plate as you cut upward towards the top of the head until the knife looks as though it is in the center or crown of the head. Keep in mind that as you complete this cut the knife needs to go deep enough to physically touch the spine of the fish without penetrating it. The spine will be your guide for the longest cut you need to make.

8. At this point, if you feel your grip on the fish is slipping, get another rag. With your knife blade sitting squarely on the fish's spine, twist the knife blade so that the sharp edge points toward the tail of the fish, with the entire blade of the knife underneath the flesh of the fish. For safety reasons, I grab the flesh on the underside of the fish and hold it up with my left hand so I can guide my knife along the spine without it getting near my hand.

9. At this stage, it's best if the blade of the knife travels along the spine of the fish as you cut the length of the body. Keep your left hand further back from the blade as you lift the flap of meat with the same hand. As the knife in your right hand moves, so should your left hand. Both should continue to perform the same function until the knife gets to the score at the tail. Aim the knife towards the score and lift the blade at an angle so that your cut will end at the beginning of the score.

10. The semi-finished product will look like the image above. The process for removal of the rib cage and fat is academic.

The cut to remove the fat should be a straight line. The removal of the ribs should be done with the blade of the knife parallel to the ribs. Starting at the top of the rib cage, closest to the spine, start to score the meat just above the bones and continue to score the meat the length of the ribs by using them as a guide until you get to the skinnier end of the fish. Go back to the top of the rib cage and repeat the process until you have removed the ribs. Repeat the entire fillet process for the other side of the fish.

With the removal of all the major bones you are free to enjoy the catch of the day any way you see fit.

Glossary

Abrasion: depletion of line strength due to nicks and frays caused by, but not limited to, rubbing up against hard objects such as rocks and tree branches.

Adipose fin: small fin on the back of a fish just forward of the caudal fin (tail).

Anal fin: located on the underbelly of fish. It is the fin between the ventral fin and the caudal fin.

Asphyxiate: to cause an extreme decrease in the amount of oxygen in the body accompanied by excess carbon dioxide leading to unconsciousness or death. Asphyxiation begins for all aquatic animals with gills the moment they are taken out of water. The main indicator is dark discoloration of the body soon after initial oxygen deprivation.

Bail: rests at the top of the reel but outside of the spool. The bail is open (flipped) by moving it up and over the spool, which allows for the line to pay out as it's cast. The bail is closed by the reverse action that allows the fisherman to retract the line by reeling the handle of the reel.

Backeddy: a pool of water that swirls in the opposite direction of the mainstream. An outcropping of land into a river that causes this holding water.

Barb: the small sharp point inthe opposite direction of the main point of a hook. Some fishing areas require that fishermen use barbless hooks. The alternative to buying barbless hooks is to pinch the barbs down with needlenose pliers.

Barometric pressure: the rising and falling of the barometer that forecasts the coming weather by either rising or falling atmospheric pressure. It's identified as high or low system that indicates clear or cloudy conditions. A low-pressure system may carry precipitation. A high-pressure system is typically void of precipitation.

Barrel swivel: a connector between lines that ties the two together by knots threaded through an eyelet at either end. The swivel action allows the line to remain stationary while the offering at the leader end spins if it needs to in order to function properly, such as with a spinner, spoon, or bladed artificial lure without causing line twist.

Beads: protective hollow devices that allow terminal gear to slide up and down a line without causing damage to it. The bead above the hook also allows spinning gear to rotate more freely without the threat of losing the lure due to abrasion.

Bite area: the space between the hook point and shank, also known as the gap. The greater the bite area, the more likely the hook-set will be deep and solid the first time a fisherman pulls back on his line.

Blank: the shaft of the fishing rod that functions as the body. It is stout and stiff at the butt area and flexible at the tip. Ordinarily the rod blank is composed of two halves.

Blood knot: combination of two lines of equal strength tied together. Used when no other line is available to replace the diminished spool capacity on the reel. The strength of the knot is about 85%.

Blown-out: refers to rivers that have

achieved an unfishable state. Blown-out rivers are high and muddy, making bank fishing virtually impossible. Though these waters can be fished successfully, it takes a great understanding of where the fish hold during these conditions.

Bobber fishing: using a floatation device to indicate when a fish has struck a jig. The fisherman knows to set the hook when the bobber submerges.

Boil: water forcibly driven towards the surface without causing it to fracture or riffle. Boils can be found in back-eddies and pools. It's commonplace for fish to hold in slow-moving water and create boils as they rise suddenly towards the surface of a river.

Bottom bouncing: a type of drift fishing done by bouncing a weight system along the riverbed. Slinky and lead weights fall to the bottom of the river and bounce along the rocks while the corkie, eggs or other bait floats above it via the leader.

Buck: a term used to describe the gender of a male fish. The upper jaw protruding past the eye identifies a buck. The lower jaw is called the mandible and kype.

Catch and release: Returning fish safely back into the water so a good brood stock is ensured for the future. This is the bedrock of good sportsman-like conduct.

Caudal fin: the caudal fin is also known as the tail. Spot identification, or lack thereof, on the tail is used to determine species of salmon.

Caudal wrist: the area between the adipose fin and the tail. For tailing purposes, it's the ideal place to grab the fish without harming it.

CFS: a type of measurement used by the United States Geological Survey charting water volume by"cubic feet per second". In conjunction with the state hatchery system this form of measurement allows them to forecast potential floods, escapement, and the return of spawning fish.

Cheater: a rotund buoyant lure made the same material as a corkie that operates under the same guidelines for distinguishing sizes. Its primary use is drift fishing.

Clinch knot: a double loop knot used primarily to tie other lines together via a swivel. The improved clinch knot may also be used to tie directly to the hook or artificial lures such as spinners and spoons.

Clippers: allow for cutting materials that cannot be cut with scissors, they provide the strength of pliers without needing to use one.

Combat fishing: the presence of many fishermen in a very small area of a river. The anomaly occurs when there is an overabundance of fish in the water. These areas are a great places for the novice to learn how to fish.

Confluence: water of various streams that come together to form one body.

Corkie: a round, rotund, or oblong floating lure that complies with non-buoyant lure restrictions. It's tied to a leader for presentation near or at the bottom of any riverbed. Corkies come in various sizes, that become smaller as the number of the size becomes smaller. A size-ten corkie is smaller than a size eight.

Dorsal fin: the major fin located on the back of most fish. The dorsal fin height is sometimes used to distinguish hatchery steelhead and natives.

Drag: resistance on a fishing reel against the pull on fishing line that pays out when a fish is hooked.

Drift mending: adjusting your mainline that rests or rises just above the surface of the water in order to take out slack that either the wind or water might create.

Egg loop: ties directly to the hook. The loop within the knot is designed to hold eggs, yarn, or other baits.

Escapement: a term used in the state hatchery system to measure the volume of fish that are tracked as they go down a river into the ocean or saltwater system.

Typically, this type of tracking is done by tagging fish when they are less than six months old. Because hydroelectric dams may be too daunting a task for zeroes (fish younger than the age of one) to traverse, barging them downriver is practiced as an alternative means of escapement.

Eye: refers to the guides on a fishing rod. They rest on both the top and bottom portions of the rod, the lower portion has the least amount of eyes.

Felt: a non-woven fabric or matted material of compressed animal fiber that may be fur or wool. It is placed on the bottom of boots that are intended for wading, and affords fishermen the ability to walk along surfaces of rocks in a river that might be covered in algae, or in water that may be too fast to traverse otherwise.

Filing: a motion that creates a sharp point on the end of a hook.

Fillet: a compact piece of boneless meat or fish. A style of fish preparation that allows the meat to be frozen for six months to a year, depending on how well the fish is processed and stored.

Fish "optical" perspective: reverse refraction of light and angle of the fish in the water presents a unique perspective on how fish perceive our image from beneath the surface of the water. The more shallow a fish is, the less it can see out of the water, conversely, the deeper it is, the greater its field of vision.

Flipping: a short reverse underhand cast that allows drift fishermen to fish in close quarters too cramped for overhand casts. Flipping can be done very close to the bank with overhanging brush.

Free-bail: a tactic to fool a large fish into stopping a strong run downstream by flipping the bail over allowing the line to pay out freely, causing a belly in the line to form, thus causing resistance in the opposite direction and making the fish believe that it needs to turn around and head back upstream.

Flossing: a term that is used when someone allows his line to drift through the water and wait for the mainline to stroke the body of a fish. When he feels the line against the fish he pulls back with a fluid motion not like that of setting the hook. The leader line then follows the mainline backwards, hooking a fish in the body or outside of the mouth.

Gear oil: a petroleum-based derivative used to aid in the lubrication of gears and bearings in a fishing reel.

Gill plate: a covering that protects the gills of a fish. The gill plates are located at the head and encompass the area from the top of the head to the lower portion of the jaw.

Gill: the respiratory organ of fish use to breathe water to obtain oxygen. The gills are found directly underneath the gill-plate.

Gilling: removal of gills from legally retained fish. Gilling allows the organs to evacuate unwanted blood for a better-tasting fillet that is not as pungent or fishy.

Gliding: a modified version of drift fishing that involves drifting the riverbed, about six inches to a foot. It allows for a quicker response from the angler when a fish disturbs the smooth presentation of the offering.

Glow ball: corkie, cheaters, spinners, or any other non-buoyant setup designed to attract fish in darkness by glowing.

Handling fish: this book promotes catch and release. When handling a fish, take care not to mortally wound a fish, with careless actions. If you don't have a cloth net in which to land a fish, then "tail" the fish while keeping its head in the water so asphyxiation does not occur. Removal of the hook should be done in such a fashion as not to cause mortal wounds around the head, jaw, and gills. The state of Washington regulation handbook states, "if you hook a fish in the tongue you should keep it if legal to do so". The mortality rate of fish that are hooked in the tongue is extremely high; putting the fish back into water is the same as putting a dead fish back into the river.

Hatchery: rearing ponds sponsored by the state in which fish eggs are harvested, incubated, hatched, and then reared for a short period of time. Upon successful maturation they are released into freshwater river systems throughout the state. Missing right ventral fins and adipose fins often identify hatchery fish. In some rare cases where marking does not take place, it is the height of the dorsal fin that distinguishes between a hatchery fish and a native.

Hats: wide-brimmed hats cool and warm the head, also aid polarized glasses by blotting out invasive light rays that interfere with their optimal function.

Hen: a term that is used to identify a female fish. The upper jaw of a female does not go past the eye. The lower jaw does not develop an overly extended "kype," like the male, during the spawning cycle.

Hit, the: also called the take, strike, or bump. It comes in various forms that many beginners do not recognize. The hit can be the line slowing down during the drift when it had not on the previous cast, or it can be that the line stops completely. It might be that the line becomes just a little bit heavier than it had from the last drift, that is to say, the line as it goes through the water neither stops or slows down rather, it seems just to move in a way that makes the water feel thicker. You can feel the difference on the line as it rests on your fingertip throughout the drift. Occasionally the hit will feel like a couple of quick taps on your line as though someone were touching the tip of your rod. Ultimately it is anything that is anomalous during the drift. To discern any discrepancy, drift through a body of

water and familiarize yourself with it in just a few minutes, when something changes in the way the line feels, or if it slows or stops, then set the hook, because only a fish can cause these changes in the way your line travels through water.

Hold: a body of water that will predictably house (hold) fish routinely. A hold can be a tailout, riffle, pool, backeddy, or slot. Most of the river will not hold fish for very long, locating these places will produce fish.

Honey hole: a secret spot that routinely holds fish. A hold that will often allow a fisherman to hook fish when just a few yards downstream no fish will bite.

Hook-set: the moment your line has stopped in the water and you pull back on your rod as hard as you can to set the hook firmly into the jaw of the fish.

Hook setup: can have a corkie, cheater, eggs, or shrimp but must have a hook, egg-loop, toothpick, or bead. The size of your setup is based on water clarity. The size of the profile is based on water clarity, volume, speed, and barometric pressure.

Hooks: refer to single, double, triple, octopus and snelled. For the purposes of this book, we refer to the single-point octopus hook for drift fishing. They come in bundles of eight, 25, 50, and 100. The regulation handbook refers to the legal size of a hook by the distance between the tine and shank.

Horse: an over-anxious fisherman attempting to land a fish prematurely by pulling on his rod and line in a way that exceeds the test capabilities of the monofilament. Most people who horse a fish end up losing them for a number of reasons, including broken line, slack, or a hook that is yanked out of the fish.

Hydroelectric dam: generates electricity by converting the energy of running water. These dams often control the level of rivers by either holding back the water in times of energy crisis, thus lowering the level of the river, or by discharging more water in times of greater rainfall and deeper snow packs, which in turn raises the level.

Hydrograph: charts the physical conditions, boundaries, flow, and related characteristics of the earth's surface waters. The USGS has websites that will direct you to hydrographs in your state. These graphs have up-to-the-hour reports that are available to the public.

Identification of fish species: an array of methodologies identify fish species predominantly through the mouth and spots along the body. Chinook have a black mouth and black gum line. Coho have a black mouth with a white gum line. Steelhead have a white mouth and white gum line. Consult your regulation handbook for clarification of species not listed.

Improved clinch knot: a double loop knot used primarily to tie other lines together via a swivel. The improved clinch knot may also be used to tie directly to the hook or artificial lures.

Invisible line: means *nearly* invisible. It is the exact opposite of a *highly visible* line. The function is to present an offering (on the leader) so that the offering looks natural enough to decieve a fish into striking at the hook.

Jetty: a small protruding landmass into a body of water that influences the current. Typically a jetty precedes a back-eddy.

Kelt: loose term to describe a steelhead that has spawned and returned to the main stream and is preparing to migrate out to sea. It is also called a punched fish. A punched fish is a hatchery fish that has a hole punched into the side of the gill plate. The meat of a kelt makes it unworthy because of the quality and texture of the meat, which in time of the actual spawning cycle diminishes dramatically and turns white.

Knots: egg loop, double clinch knot, and blood knot are the main knots drift fishermen uses. The egg loop is found on the hook, the clinch knot can be found on the swivel, the blood knot connects two lines that are short to make one long one.

Kype: part of a fish's jaw that protrudes out, down (upper jaw), and upward (lower jaw). The kype of a male fish is usually more pronounced than that of the female. Chum salmon have the most pronounced jaw during the spawning cycle of the species of fish that migrate from salt to fresh water.

Lateral line: a series of sensory pores along the head and sides of a of fish by which water current, vibration, and pressure changes are perceived. The smallest physical interference with the lateral line will eventually kill a fish, given the vital nature of its ability to locate food and avoid predators.

Leader: monofilament line that travels from a swivel to the hook. The length of the leader is determined by natural conditions that include barometric pressure, water current, water height, speed, temperature, and water clarity.

Leader holder: flexible tubing that is found in most hardware stores in the plumbing section. The holder is non-abrasive and easily stored. Leaders are wound around the tubing starting with the tag end of the line and finishing with the hook setup.

License: indicates what species of fish or animal you are legally able to keep. The tracking system of the license allows for quick verification of legal fishermen.

Line test: monofilament strength is based on pound resistance against it to its breaking point. If the line is six-pound test, then six pounds is its limit against the pull of a fish. If the resistance goes past six pounds, then the line will break.

Line twist: twisting action of a line as it is transferred from one spool to the next, causing it to tangle around itself making it very difficult for distance casting and reeling line back onto the spool. It also occurs when the strain of a fish stretches the line and the line does not return to its original form. This kind of twisting is called "memory". The counter spin that is provided by a barrel or snap swivel, allows the ability of the line to untangle itself.

Line viscosity: an indicator that line lies somewhere between a solid and a liquid. Monofilament is gelatinous, Allowing the line to stretch without breaking when it is stretched violently. Viscosity is also known as line test.

Line-belly: formed when the wind catches fishing line as it is cast. Belly in the line makes it difficult for the angler to sense a strike. Line-belly can form in water that travels at two separate speeds in the same area. That is to say, the surface water may travel at a speed greater or less than the water underneath it. This causes the leader to fall behind the terminal gear or to float further in front of it causing the line to form a belly.

Line memory: twisting of line that occurs from a brand-new spool of line. The twisting can cause the line to spring off the spool, creating tangles. The way to prevent line memory is to reel in line from a storage spool in the same direction of your reel spool. When using a leader with line memory, stroke the line with your index and forefinger, then pull it with your left hand for the length of the leader. This process assumes that the line is in your right hand. This technique takes out the curling that occurs from having your line on a leader holder.

Mainline: main body of line that pays off of the spool when cast out into water. Typically the mainline is somewhat stronger than the leader. Because the mainline is stronger the leader should break at the knot, allowing the fisherman

to preserve his mainline and save most of the terminal gear when it is caught on a snag.

Monofilament: a strand of synthetic line used for fishing. Neither truly solid or liquid, rather a very strong gelatinous line is capable of withstanding the setting power of a fisherman and the strike of a fish, if the strength of the line complements the species of fish.

Mouthed: an offering that has been almost imperceptibly touched by the mouth of a fish as it drifts through the river. A steelhead will take ane offering into its mouth and then move backwards in the water with it, simultaneously turn with it and let it go. It is said that steelhead are fastidious and will clean the area they occupy, clearing it of debris.

Native: that species of fish that is not hatched or reared by the state hatchery system. Natives tend to be stronger fighters than their hatchery counterparts and over a period time they become larger and stronger than reared fish.

Natural presentation: accomplished when a reel is "free-bailed", allowing the offering to drift down river "naturally".

Needlenose pliers: pointed pliers that blunt at the end. Needlenose pliers can be used for cutting toothpicks and lead. They are also used to remove hooks from fish and other objects, and are used for the preparation of slinky and other weight systems.

Netting: landing a fish. Netting implies that the user knows that to successfully net a fish you must aim the fish's head at the net as it swims towards it, then raise the net once the fish is inside it. Be sure that you get the fish into it without touching the hook or you stand the strong possibility of losing the fish.

Offering: describes what is on or near your hook. It is your choice of drift gear that has been dictated by observing weather conditions, barometric pressure,

91

section of the river, water clarity, and human presence.

Okies: a type of corkie in the shape of a cluster of eggs. They are highly buoyant and are a good alternative to the corkie when the bite is off. The placement of the okie is the same as a corkie.

Olfactory: relating to the sense of smell. Steelhead are renowned for their sense of smell. It has been estimated that their capability is five thousand times that of a human. Much of its brain is dedicated to this function. Bear in mind, they are highly instinctive and survive by adapting in a very short period of time. This is abundantly clear when fishermen pressure the fish and they stop biting.

Pectoral fins: the two most forward fins on the underbelly of a fish.

Pencil lead: a weight system for riverbeds made of gravel and sand. The sizes vary between 1/16 to 1/4 inches in diameter. A hole is punched into them or rubber tubing placed over pencil lead so it can be attached to a swivel and then tied together with the mainline and leader.

Plunking: setup includes a mainline, three-way swivel, and a dropper line. The best time to plunk is during high, muddy water.

Poaching: taking fish illegally, that is to say, not complying within the parameters of the guidelines set down from the fish and game department delegated throughout the regulation handbook for the state within one wishes to fish. Snagging is poaching.

Pocket fishing: fast-moving water over boulders and structure in a small area in a larger body of water. You need a heavier weight to get down to these areas, but they do hold fish now and again. They are resting areas for fish as they migrate up the river.

Polarized glasses: refract ultra-violet rays and diminish glare. They are excellent for visibility in a high-pressure system. Polarized glasses are a must for spotting fish.

Pool: an area of water that has deepened and slows down near the bed of the river, creating a place for fish to rest. Drifting very light weight, spoon fishing, or bobber fishing are productive. Plunking is also an option.

Presentation: how your offering reaches fish . Presentations differ by the offering, weight system, how far you cast out, and how far you drift upstream from your position.

Probing: a form of fishing that allows you to fish a great deal of the water in an accelerated amount of time when river systems are between seasons. It involves casting out into the water based on its clarity. If the visibility is two feet then your second drift will be two feet further than your first one, and the third cast will be another two feet and you continue on from there. If the water clarity is three feet then your cast difference will be three feet; if it is six then you will cast every six feet.

Punch card: an area of the fishing license that documents the zoned area, amount, and type of fish that you caught and retained legally.

Punched fish: steelhead that have spawned and been identified and recorded have a hole punched safely into their gill plating and are then transported a short distance downriver to be released. The quality of the fish's meat is poor at this stage. Though they will strike at almost anything, the meat texture is so bad that it falls apart in loose shreds as you try to prepare it for consumption or transportation. Punched fish should be placed back in the water so the recovery time will make it a better fish to fight eat at a later date.

Raingear: anything that protects you from a cold and wet environment; such as Micromesh, Gortex, or any other clothing that allows your body to breath and stay dry at the same time.

Reading the water: the ability to look at the surface of water and determine where fish are holding.

Recon: an advanced trip to an area you want to fish, to check out the water and terrain before you fish it. Recon ensures that you are familiar enough with the terrain in all seasons to fish safely.

Redd: an area of the riverbed where steelhead and salmon spawn. It is identified by undulations of gravel in slower-moving water.

Reel: that portion of gear that sits attached at the bottom of the rod.

Refraction: the displacement of light rays through a prism. In this case it refers to water and the perception of objects as seen through the surfacer. Refraction causes images to appear in places they are not, that is to say, the rock or fish you see in the water may not be as big or as close as you might think. The refractive ability of the water surface distorts the location and relative sizes of the objects.

Regulation handbook: rules and regulations that legally define the parameters of fishing behavior for each state.

Replica: using plaster, an artist can replicate trophy fish instead of stuffing and mounting the body of a fish. Replication assures that the trophy will last far longer and remain more appealing visually.

Riffle: provides cover for fish when the barometric pressure is high. The water tends to move fast, which causes the surface to flutter over shallow water and rocks. Fish gravitate to these areas that are deep enough to hold them. A riffle can be found below a tailout or pool.

Rod butt: the lower half of the rod where the reel is placed. The purpose of the rod butt is to give the fisherman a place for his forearm, to better assist him while he is fighting a fish. The butt functions as a lever when fighting a fish, when you set

your hook, the butt of the rod should be in alignment with your forearm so that when you set the hook the butt of the rod is firmly against your forearm giving the leverage that you need to secure the hookset one time.

Roe: the eggs of a female fish. Roe comes in skeins holding thousands of eggs.

Run: slang term for a migration of fish that intend to spawn.

Saltfish: term discerning how long a fish has been to sea. Most fishermen agree that a fish that ranges from six to eight pounds is a two-salt fish meaning that it is about three years old. A four-saltfish would be about five years old and weigh ten to twelve pounds. When you hear about saltfish, add one year to the life of the fish because it takes a rainbow trout about a year to go to sea and when it returns it is referred to as a steelhead.

Scale: the outer layer of a fish. The scales have growth rings that can only be seen through a microscope. Like a tree, growth rings indicate how old the fish is. The growth rings provide hatcheries with invaluable data as to how long a species of fish stays out to sea; this in turn allows for an element of predictable forecasts as both salmon and steelhead return to spawn.

When a fish loses a scale it creates a hole in its defense system, which can cause infection and death. These infections can manifest themselves with swim bladder disease or constipation. Inflammation can cause irreparable damage to the lateral line. The lateral line helps fish locate food and sense predators.

The color of the scales range from black to chrome, and the entire spectrum in between, depending on the species and the time of year.

Seam: the line where two currents/bodies of water meet. An ideal place for fish to hold while waiting for food to flow down river.

Setting the hook: the action taken to solidly plant a hook into the jaw of a fish by the quick pulling action of a rod when the fisherman has an indication that a fish has picked up his offering. The hookset generally needs to be set once to secure the fish.

Shank: the longest and straightest part of the hook. It starts at the eye and travels downward until it begins to bend.

Shaker: an immature fish that has sexually developed. A shaker can range from two pounds to ten depending on the species of fish.

Skein: the membrane that surrounds unfertilized roe. It is widely thought that female fish that jump out of the water and land on the surface on the sides of their bodies are attempting to break up the skein to free her eggs for spawning purposes. There is no scientific data that substantiates the claim.

Slab: refers to an uncommonly large fish.

Slinky: a weight system that consists of parachute chord that holds lead shot of various sizes. The slinky is generally used when the bed of a river is comprised of boulders, or in other snag-riddled areas. The premise of the slinky is that it "slink" over structures without the line and weight becoming snagged.

Slot: typically found above a tailout. Imagine the bed of a river as made up of hills and valleys. The hills represent shallower and faster water, and the valleys represent deeper and slower water. Fish gravitate towards the slower water. Slots are the fishable areas that look as though they are actually fast on the surface of the river. To identify the slot look for water that undulates back and forth with slick or smoother water on either side of it.

Smoking: a process of curing fish by placing it in a smoker that slowly burns wood chips. Typically the fish is filleted, keeping the skin on one side intact, soaked in brine, and then placed into a smoker. The type of wood chips used designate the overall flavor. The meat becomes edible after a few hours of slow cooking.

Snagging: intentionally or unintentionally hooking a fish anywhere but in its mouth. This is illegal.

Snap swivel: a barrel swivel with a clip attached to one end of the barrel. A barrel swivel has two eyes and a centerpiece of an oval shape. Both of the barrel swivel's eyes spin 360 degrees to prevent line twists. The snap portion of the swivel is made up of a hook that folds into a clip that holds the hook of the snap in place. The function of the snap swivel is to replace and hold your weight system for easy insertion and removal of slinky and pencil lead.

Spawn: to create fertilized eggs in large numbers during migratory cycles. It is the contribution of genetic material from both the male and female to produce offspring. The cycle includes the development of redds in gravel riverbeds that hold vast numbers of eggs. Typically the female digs out the redd and then buries the fertilized eggs before going out to sea.

Spinners: any kind of lure that rotates in the water to attract fish. A spinner can be a rooster-tail or a vibrax. There are corkie-like spinners designed to attract steelhead in water that has very little water clarity. It's the action of the spinner spinning that gets the fish's attention, but the color and size dictates whether or not the fish will strike your lure.

Spool: holds your line static so you may utilize it when needed. A spool is found either at the top of your reel, or a spool of line separate from your reel, which holds line for storage purposes only.

Spotting fish: a fisherman's ability to read water successfully and locate fish. Spotting fish means that a fisherman has the ability to discern water height, speed, depth, temperature, and flow in order to understand the location of fish.

Springer: refers to fish that migrate from salt to fresh water. The migration typically occurs in March and ends in August. The biggest run of springers is from May to July, depending on the system you are fishing. They have been known to run as late as October and early November. Though springers are fewer and farther between than their counterpart, the winter run, they are renowned for the fights and the bites which are both considerably more aggressive than steelhead caught in the winter.

Stringer: anything that can be placed through the gill-plate and lower jaw to restrict the motion of legally retained fish.

Tag: defines the end of a fishing line. Tags are usually cut very short to prevent tangles.

Tailing: a technique for landing fish with a gloved or bare hand. It is a way for fishermen to release fish back into the water without causing harm. Tailing involves grabbing a fish by the caudal wrist of the tail. It is the area of the fish located between the adipose fin and the tail, which is also called the caudal fin. Grabbing the fish in this area incapacitates it substantially, allowing the fisherman to safely release it back into the water. When tailing fish, it is best not to lift it out of the water while, at the same time, leaving the head, including the gills, under the surface.

Tailout: a section of a river just after a pool and just above a riffle. It is a resting place for fish that have just come in from fast-moving water (riffle).

Tail walking: when a hooked fish jumps out of the water and uses its tail to propel itself along the surface of the water in an effort to throw the hook out of its jaw.

Terminal gear: found at the end of the mainline and the beginning of the leader, and includes the barrel swivel, snap swivel, bumper, bead, and weight system.

Thermometers: a tool for measuring the water temperature, and play a critical role in understanding the activity of fish. The colder the water, the more lethargic the fish, and the warmer the water, the more active they tend to be.

Tine: the portion of the hook that is inserted into the jaw of the fish as the hook is set. It is a single prong that is very sharp.

Tributary: a juncture where a smaller stream pours into a larger one. It is also a stream that pours into an estuary or marine water. Tributaries typically form seams that hold fish.

USGS: United States Geological Survey is a resource management designated by the Federal Government to work with many water management installations throughout the United States.

Ventral fin: is the set of fins that lie between the pectoral and anal fins located around the abdominal-pelvic area of fish. Most fish with their right ventral fin removed are to be put back into the water in which they were hooked.

Visible line: highly visible line that is easily seen by fishermem as it travels through the drift. Visible line allows fishermen to ascertain, visually is a fish has disturbed the leader by watching it hesitate during the drift. The mainline is the only portion of line that should be visible. A visible leader will spook fish away from the offering at the hook.

Waders: waterproof hip boots or chest waders that allow a fisherman to wade across rivers and/or fish in the water without getting wet or cold. Wear waders with felt when river rocks are covered in algae.

Water clarity: the ability to see through the water. The depth at which you are able to see into the water measures visibility. If you are able to see the bed of the river clearly, it's called gin-clear or unlimited.

Water current: the rate at which water travels. The United States Geological

Survey has a rating system known as "CFS", or cubic feet per second, that determines the rate of speed a river travels. The currents of various systems throughout the United States are accessible by typing in the key word hydrograph on your browser when on the Internet. The data that is provided by the USGS is updated by the hour on most "real-time" systems.

Water height: relates to the shoreline of a river. Water height is closely related to a hydrograph, flood warnings are issued for waters that achieve too much elevation. The depth (water height) of a river is a variable that indicates whether or not a system is fishable.

Water temperature: is found by using a floating thermometer specifically designed for field use. The temperature verifies the lethargy or activity of fish.

Winter run: identify fish that migrate up river systems in November and continue until late February and into early March. The winter run of steelhead is far and away more lethargic than the summer run, but the numbers of fish make that run more attractive to fishermen despite the inhospitable conditions of the cold weather. Because the winter run is focused on spawning, the fish are more apt to be spooked and less inclined to strike any offering.

Yarn: continuous strand of fiber made up of natural or synthetic material. It is sometimes placed on the egg loop of a hook to hold scent longer for artificial lures. It is thought that yarn also tangles in the teeth of steelhead and salmon, giving extra time to the fisherman to react and set the hook.